CONEY ISLAND

QUALITY

Geo. C. Tilyou's
STEEPLECHASE PARK
Coney Island, N. Y.

Is the largest and the most completely equipped FUN FACTORY in the world.

Containing 2 SWIMMING POOLS, OCEAN BATHING BEACH, BALL ROOM, ROLLER SKATING RING, besides THE GREAT PAVILION OF FUN.

115157

POST CARD

THIS SPACE FOR ADDRESS ONLY

A
POSTCARD JOURNEY
TO THE
CITY OF FIRE

CONEY

ISLAND

A
POSTCARD JOURNEY
TO THE
CITY OF FIRE

RICHARD SNOW

DESIGN
KIYOSHI KANAI

BRIGHTWATERS PRESS

Printed in the United States of America

Library of Congress Catalogue Number: 84-071458

ISBN 0-918305-01-2

Brightwaters Press
200 East 61st Street
New York, New York 10021

For Geoffrey and Jillian, who have been with me to so many of the far-flung outposts of the old imperial Coney—the mill-chute ride at Rochester, the roller coaster in the trees at Erie, the derelict Whip outside of Johnstown—and for William, who has already solemnly braved the B & B Carousell at Coney itself.

Coney Island is the Tom-Tom of America. Every nation has, and needs—and loves—its Tom-Tom. It has its needs of orgiastic escape from respectability—that is, from the world of What-we-have-to-do into the world of What-we-would-like-to-do, from the world of duty that endureth forever into the world of joy that is permitted for a moment. . . .

It is of no use to criticize humanity. Like all creations, it—survives its critics. The only interesting thing is to try to understand it, or, at least, appreciate. Perhaps Coney Island is the most human thing that God ever made, or permitted the devil to make.

—Richard Le Gallienne, 1905

INTRODUCTION

"If Paris is France," George C. Tilyou wrote in 1886, "then Coney Island, between June and September, is the world." This boast appeared in the sole issue of "Tilyou's Real Estate Telephone," a four-page newspaper filled with just that sort of hyperbole: the fact that shooting galleries were up for rent a few hundred yards west of where they usually were located was disclosed under the headline "Westward Ho!" So Tilyou's claim for the universality of his scrubby sandspit might seem to be just more commercial bombast. But in fact, Tilyou was right— or would be. In the next twenty years Coney Island was to become the most famous resort in the world, a carnival grand enough to draw visitors from Europe and send them away happy, and a place that, for a little while, so perfectly reflected the national mood that its sideshows and theatricals were nothing less than a prophecy of how the twentieth century would unfold.

George C. Tilyou himself had something to do with this transformation; and so, too, did Coney Island's location. It lay at the foot of Brooklyn, nine miles from Manhattan, a narrow sandbar five miles long and, for most of its career, a place of windy desolation. A shell road had connected it with Long Island as early as 1829, and a few wealthy Brooklynites trickled out during cholera seasons to put up in a small hotel called the Coney Island House. By the time of the Civil War there were a dozen hotels, some bathhouses and chowder stands, and a growing conviction on the part of local entrepreneurs that the place could develop into a spa on the order of Newport. There were few immediate signs of this transformation, however: when one reporter went out to have a look during the height of the 1870 season, he came upon a sign that said "Bathers Without Full Suits Positively Prohibited by Law," and, beneath this strict injunction, the rotting carcasses of a dog and a horse.

Still, the island was becoming more cosmopolitan. In the 1870s three huge frame hotels went up— the Oriental, the Manhattan Beach, and the Brighton Beach. Railroad lines ran south to serve them, and in 1880 the Iron Steamboat Company started running a fleet of handsome little walking-beam steamers from Manhattan.

And Coney was beginning to get a taste of the fantastic architecture that would flourish there in the next quarter century. At first the buildings were relatively straightforward: Brazilian and Japanese pavilions from the Centennial Exhibition that had just been held in Philadelphia. But then someone decided it would be a good idea to build a hotel in the shape of an elephant, and up it went. One-hundred fifty feet from toenail to howdah, the tin-clad wooden beast contained thirty-four rooms and a sizable dance hall. At night its eyes glowed yellow above the bathhouses and band shells and carousels. Complex, facetious, and a little sinister, it was an augury.

Along with these early attractions came prostitutes, pickpockets, three-card monte men. Coney lay outside the jurisdiction of Manhattan and Brooklyn, under the rule of John Y. McKane. A hard-handed sometime carpenter, McKane simultaneously occupied every post of importance in the local government from Chief of Police to Superintendent of Sunday Schools. Nobody opened so much as a hot-corn stand without his approval. "Houses of prostitution are a necessity on Coney Island," he said; so, too, were gambling and con games, as long as they were more or less restricted to the rowdy western end of the island. Coney was gaining a reputation gamy enough to stir denunciation from indignant townships in the

Middle West. It made no difference how often John Philip Sousa spent the summer there playing to irreproachable middle-class audiences, Coney Island was Sodom. In fact, according to Thomas DeQuincey Tully, secretary of the Law and Order Society, "Sodom was not a circumstance to the sin-debauched and crime-soaked Coney Island."

That reputation never really went away, but McKane did. The reform movement of the early 1890s rolled over Coney. McKane stood against it for a while—"injunctions don't go here," he said as he jailed poll watchers—but in the end they got him. In 1894, he went to Sing Sing.

McKane's departure allowed George C. Tilyou to emerge from mercantile exile. Tilyou's was a family of profound antiquity by Coney Island standards; his parents had moved there when he was three years old in 1865 to establish the Surf House, which sold Bavarian Lager for five cents a glass and rented "Fancy Flannel Bathing Suits." When the Centennial brought crowds east, some spilled over from Philadelphia onto Coney's beaches, where the fourteen-year-old George Tilyou found he could sell them souvenir bottles of salt water and cigar boxes full of sand for a quarter apiece. "For my first day's labor," he said, "I realized $13.45, which seemed to me a fortune, so I immediately retired." He came out of retirement two years later to start a stage line on the island's western end, and by the time he was twenty he was running Tilyou's Surf Theater, which, he was proud to recall, brought "the first painted scenery" to the island. Then he went up against McKane, testified in court, and promptly lost his real estate holdings. Deprived of his livelihood, he never considered leaving Coney—and, in fact, couldn't: there were days, he said, when he didn't have the carfare to get to Brooklyn.

But with McKane in prison, Tilyou was free to operate the way he wanted to. He had been to the 1893 World's Columbian Exposition—the Chicago World's Fair—and there saw the great Ferris Wheel. He tried to buy it, learned that it was already promised to St. Louis for the 1904 fair, and returned to Coney, where he ordered a wheel half the size and blithely claimed, "On this site will be built the largest Ferris Wheel in the world." By the time the wheel arrived from the Pennsylvania Steel Company, he had sold enough nearby concession space to pay for it.

By the end of the summer Tilyou was in good shape and thinking about building other rides. In the meantime, Captain Paul Boyton, who had made quite a name for himself by bobbing across the English Channel in an inflated rubber suit, opened his Sea Lion Park near the elephant hotel. The park contained a number of attractions, chief among them the Shoot the Chutes, a water slide down which passengers scudded in flat-bottomed boats out into an artificial lagoon. The ride was a great success, but it was Boyton's park itself that interested Tilyou.

The prostitutes and con men had not decamped with McKane, and Tilyou believed the island's reputation was keeping away a middle-class clientele that had money to spend. Enclose your park, and you could keep out troublemakers.

Tilyou cast around for an attraction to rival Boyton's chutes, and found it in an English ride which simulated a horserace. Since Coney Island had three real racecourses, this seemed appropriate, and in 1897 Tilyou brought the novelty to America and opened Steeplechase Park. Ringed by the ride's undulant iron tracks, the fourteen-acre park was a success from the beginning. "Coney," proclaimed a guidebook, "has risen sphinx-like from the ashes."

As Steeplechase prospered, its owner kept on the lookout for new attractions, and at the 1901 Pan-American Exposition in Buffalo he found a spectacular one: a trip to the moon operated by Fred Thompson and Elmer Dundy. Tilyou invited the showmen to bring it to Steeplechase, and it did so well that the next season they moved out, bought Boyton's Sea Lion Park, rebuilt it, and in the spring of 1903 opened Luna Park.

At first, Thompson and Dundy's advertising copy tried to pretend that Luna was another world's fair, but before long they realized it was something better, an "electric Eden" unlike anything that had ever been built before.

Luna Park was the architecture of exhilaration: its lath-and-plaster minarets were designed solely to startle and delight. The author Albert Bigelow Paine watched dusk fall on Luna and wrote, "Tall towers that had grown dim suddenly broke forth in electric outlines and gay rosettes of color, as the living spark of light traveled hither and thither, until the place was transformed into an enchanted garden, of such a sort as Aladdin never dreamed."

Beneath those blazing spires, people could shoot the chutes, ride scenic railways, and see a full-rigged circus, but it was always the spectacle of the park itself that set the mood. This was not an accident: Thompson, who had a fair amount of architectural training, thought it all out carefully. "In building for a festive occasion," he wrote, "there should be an absolute departure from all set forms of architecture. . . . [The architect] must dare to decorate a minaret with Renaissance detail or to jumble Romanesque with *l'art nouveau*, always with the idea of keeping his line constantly varied, broken, and moving, so that it may lead gracefully into the towers and minarets of a festive skyline. . . . I have tried to make [Luna Park] as much a part of the carnival spirit as the bands, flags, rides, and lights. I have tried to keep it active, mobile, free, graceful, and attractive."

The attempt was such a success that the next season a group of financiers invited Thompson to bring his giddy architecture into the heart of New York City in the form of the Hippodrome Theater. And at the same time the civic architecture of New York— the tall, white, Beaux-Arts American Renaissance buildings with their reverence for the classical past— were, in a sense, going out to Coney. Led by J. R.

Reynolds, a sometime state senator and real estate promoter, a consortium of investors decided to go Luna one better. Their park would have a million electric lights to Luna's 250,000, two chutes to Luna's one, a central tower that, at 375 feet, stood nearly 200 feet taller than Luna's. The buildings would be pure white, a sort of permanent world's fair inspired by the vast, sugar-white classical vistas of the World's Columbian Exposition. This chaste enterprise was christened Dreamland, and it was just as grand as its backers has envisaged. But perhaps it was a bit too literal, too closely wedded to the cultivated tradition. In any event, Dreamland never managed to generate quite as much popular enthusiasm as its raucous cousin Luna.

With the completion of this last park in 1904, Coney reached the peak of its efflorescence. Running full-throttle on a hot summer Sunday, the island could shuttle 300,000 people through its plazas and alleys, stuff them with fried meat and candy, turn them upside down, set them dancing to a score of bands, and send them home sunburned and groggy and half stupefied with the din of the shooting galleries and the barkers.

Those weary revelers dozing on the homebound trains had also, many of them, enjoyed in that most crowded place an intimacy unavailable anywhere else. Coney's clang and glitter always had a current of sexuality running through it. "Will she throw her arms around your neck and yell?" read the advertisement for the Cannon Coaster. "Well, I guess yes!" Tilyou knew why people liked his Steeplechase Ride. "The young men (and every man is young when there is a woman in the case) like it, because it gives them a chance to hug the girls; the girls (and every women is a girl when there is a man in the case) like it, because it gives them a chance to get hugged." Tilyou filled his park with rides that tumbled couples into each other's arms, and always there was the flash of ankle as young women swung their legs across the wooden horses.

Best of all, this casually bestowed license was entirely legitimate. Few of the couples who shrieked and clutched each other on the high turns of the Drop the Dip would have entered the ride had it been called the Whirlpool of Sensuality. But the park owners saw to it that there was reassuring evidence of uplift everywhere. Not far from the hug-inducing Steeple-chase horses, for instance, couples could calm

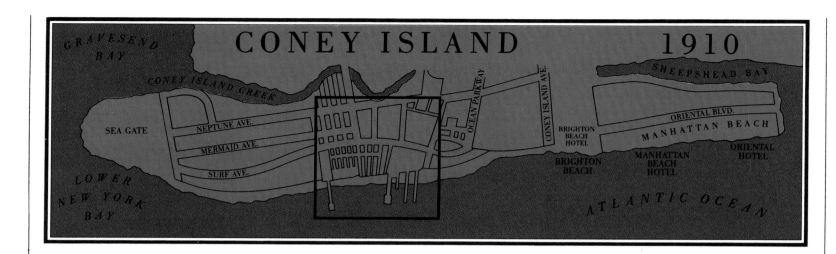

CONEY ISLAND 1910

GRAVESEND BAY

CONEY ISLAND CREEK

SEA GATE

NEPTUNE AVE.

MERMAID AVE.

SURF AVE.

LOWER NEW YORK BAY

OCEAN PARKWAY

CONEY ISLAND AVE.

SHEEPSHEAD BAY

ORIENTAL BLVD.

MANHATTAN BEACH

BRIGHTON BEACH HOTEL

BRIGHTON BEACH

MANHATTAN BEACH HOTEL

ORIENTAL HOTEL

ATLANTIC OCEAN

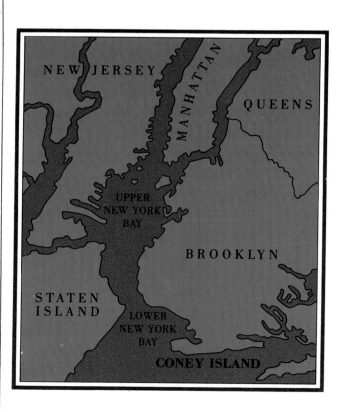

NEW JERSEY

MANHATTAN

QUEENS

UPPER NEW YORK BAY

BROOKLYN

STATEN ISLAND

LOWER NEW YORK BAY

CONEY ISLAND

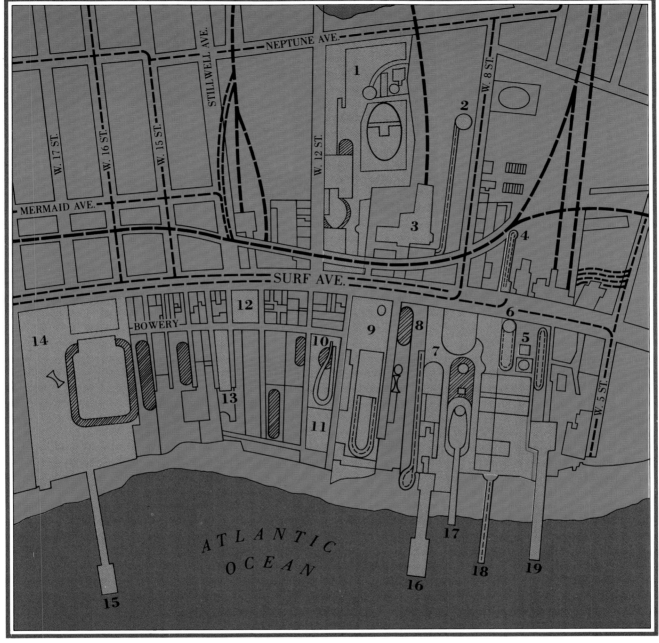

1. LUNA PARK
2. L.A. THOMPSON RAILWAY
3. SEA BEACH PALACE
4. ROCKY ROAD TO DUBLIN
5. OBSERVATION TOWER
6. PIKE'S PEAK RAILWAY

7. DREAMLAND
8. LOOP THE LOOP
9. FELTMAN'S
10. ROUGH RIDERS
11. WARD'S BATHING PAVILION
12. HENDERSON'S MUSIC HALL
13. STAUCH'S DANCE HALL

14. STEEPLECHASE PARK
15. STEEPLECHASE PIER
16. DREAMLAND PIER
17. DREAMLAND CHUTES
18. LEAP FROG RAILROAD
19. NEW IRON PIER

themselves in the park's electric plant, whose "ceiling and walls are covered with costly oil paintings depicting historical electrical events from time of Franklin and Morse and studded with jewels," and whose "engines and dynamos are enameled in white with gold mountings. A Vernis-Martin curio table holds the tools, and a beautiful mosaic table, the oil cups." The engineer moved among his dynamos clad in an immaculate duck jacket twinkling with brass buttons. He wore white gloves. "He is a college graduate, qualified to lecture upon his plant as well as to operate it."

This Fabergé egg of a generating plant may have been artificial, but then all the pleasures of this new Coney Island were, to a degree, artificial. Machines made the fun here. That, in itself, may have had a potent appeal. People who were struggling to cope with growing technological complexities in their jobs could spend an afternoon with the tables turned: at Coney, the machinery worked to divert them. Electricity whisked them through spackle grottoes where scenes lit up, and highly sophisticated theatrical technology made possible recreations of the eruption of Mount Pelée or the Johnstown flood,

and such bellicose fantasies as Luna's War of the Worlds, in which the American fleet steamed forth to sink everybody else's. In a decade, these elaborate mechanical diversions completely changed the nature of a day at Coney Island. Now people came to one of the finest beaches on the Atlantic coast and never even thought of going swimming; they might catch only a quick blue flash of ocean over the park wall before the roller coaster plunged.

There were those who saw in the frantic rhythms of all this manufactured fun the continuation of a dehumanizing process begun on the factory floor. A people who took such pleasure in being pummeled by machines were a people whose sensibilities were being narrowed and coarsened.

Maxim Gorky found Coney Island in 1906 a "slimy marsh of boredom" where "scoundrels, swept together by the dirty broom of tedium . . . creep along with weary faces and colorless eyes" while all around them "mean panderers to debased tastes unfold the disgusting nakedness of their falsehood" and "the cold gleam of the dead fire bares the stupidity of it all. Its pompous glitter rests upon everything 'round about the people."

Nevertheless, it *did* glitter. Even Gorky, aflame with his sententious loathing, was enthralled by his first sight of Coney: "Thousands of ruddy sparks glimmer in the darkness, limning in fine, sensitive outline on the black background of the sky, shapely towers of miraculous castles, palaces and temples. Golden gossamer threads tremble in the air. They intertwine in transparent, flaming patterns, which flutter and melt away in love with their own beauty mirrored in the waters. Fabulous and beyond conceiving, ineffably beautiful, is this fiery scintillation."

The American critic James Huneker didn't like Coney much better than Gorky did. He hated the people ("Unlike Sodom, Coney Island can boast at least ten good inhabitants—but they only serve to set off the repulsive qualities of their neighbours") and what happened to them there: "Every device imaginable by which man may be separated from his dimes without adequate return is in operation. You . . . go into funny houses—oh, the mockery of the title!—and later are tumbled into the open, insulted, mortified, disgusted, angry and—laughing."

Adrift in this "desperately depressing" place, Huneker nonetheless found himself, like Gorky, compelled to acknowledge its beauty. "The view of Luna Park . . . suggests a cemetery of fire, the tombs, turrets, and towers illuminated, and mortuary shafts of flame. . . . Dreamland . . . stands a dazzling apparition for men on ships and steamers out at sea. Everything is fretted with fire. Fire delicately etches some fairy structure; fire outlines an Oriental gateway; fire runs like a musical scale through many octaves. . . ."

In our time we have seen man-made spectacles bigger and brighter than Huneker's incandescent Coney, and yet the place still exercises a dim power over us. In the first flow of spring, a good many New Yorkers feel the tug of Coney Island, even if they never go there anymore. And out in the Midwest, you'll find roadside stands promising "Real Coney Island Hot Dogs." They are summoning a ghost to sell those hot dogs, and that ghost is the fleeting initial impression that comes to most of us when we hear the words "Coney Island." Never mind how well you know what a sink the place has become—the Coney Island of memory is the same one that forced Huneker into reluctant admission of its splendor.

That Coney has vanished almost without a trace, but it survives in a vast literature of picture postcards. It is fitting that this medium of mass communication should document the great, inaugural complex of mass amusement, for the postcard vogue grew with the island itself.

In 1898 the government made it legal for commercially printed postcards to go through the mails for a penny instead of two cents. Companies started turning out picture postcards, and people began collecting them. In a few years they had become a business of astonishing proportions. Americans bought 770,500,000 cards in 1906; in 1913 they mailed just slightly under a billion. No town was too modest to have a half-dozen views of its main street on sale in the general store—even if the general store was the town's only building. Naturally, then, so grand an attraction as Coney Island was covered exhaustively: 200,000 cards were mailed from Coney on a single day in early September of 1906. Nobody knows how many different views of the place were manufactured in the years before the First World War, but the number runs well up into the thousands.

Once the scenes were photographed, they often went to Germany for tinting, and many of the views of Coney Island show not what the colors of the place actually were, but what an artisan in Frankfurt thought they should be. Nevertheless, the cards are accurate in spirit: the colors tend to be startling; the night skies are rich and turbulent and a little menacing, and very black above the glare of the lights.

The cards in this book all were published between the turn of the century and the First World War. With their fierce, spurious colors and inexhaustible willingness to show alike the tallest minaret and most meager sideshow, they are the best and truest record we have of Coney Island at its tawdry, cunning, magnificent zenith.

7837. CONEY ISLAND STEAMER.

The steamer *Cepheus* heads for Coney in this 1904 view. She was owned by the Iron Steamboat Company, which operated a squadron of sturdy little excursion boats, all of them ennobled with classical names: *Cetus*, *Cygnus*, *Pegasus*, *Sirius*. They were the best way to go.

"Coney Island," said *Scientific American*, "that marvelous city of lath and burlap, should always be approached by the sea, as then, and then only, can the beauty of this ephemeral Venice be appreciated." The railroads got there faster, but they ran through a dispiriting landscape of coalyards and soap factories and ashpits and scruffy fields empty save for signs promising that "delightful suburban villas" would grow there someday. The boat ride, on the other hand, was a pleasure from the moment the steamer left the pier. "It is a rare trip down the bay in sunny summer weather," wrote Albert Bigelow Paine, "with just enough breeze to make everybody happy. Children romped up and down the upper decks, and women in fresh, cool summer wear found comfort in camp-chairs. . . . Big steamers, little tugs, handsome yachts, and white-sailed vessels all were of interest on a day like that, with the special attraction of a great ocean liner sweeping grandly out to sea, leaving its long drifting banner of smoke behind.

"Then the Island rose up out of the sea—a horizon of towers, domes, spidery elevations, and huge revolving wheels."

LANDING IRON PIER CONEY ISLAND, N. Y.

The Iron Steamers landed at Iron Pier, a relic of the Coney of a generation before.

The "steamer, flags flying," wrote a visitor, "made fast at the wharf, and from the Sabbath quietude of the sea, with its occasional winging note of a bell-buoy, we were plunged into a pudding of people."

After running a gauntlet of importuning vendors selling tin-type badges, pails and shovels, taffy, clams, and fried crabs, the excursionists could escape into the island.

Visitors who wanted to try to orient themselves instead of just wading into the chowder of brightly colored, disconnected events that was Coney's specialty would head for the Observation Tower, the tall, skeletal structure to the right. Made for the 1876 Centennial Exhibition, the three-hundred-foot tower was taller than any building in Manhattan when it arrived from Philadelphia in 1881. Its steam elevators lifted people to the best vantage point on the island.

70-40

24

Looking west from West Tenth Street: the red-roofed half-timbered buildings in the foreground are part of Feltman's enormous restaurant and beer garden; beyond the trellising of roller coasters is the long, glass-covered shed of Steeplechase Park; and at the left bathers stand in the Atlantic in front of Ward's Bathing Pavilion.

12716—Bird's-eye View, Coney Island.

Still looking west, this time from the Observation Tower along Surf Avenue, Coney's main drag: the nearest cross street is West Eighth, and the roller coaster that runs alongside it is L. A. Thompson's Scenic Railway. The domes and spires of Luna Park rise toward the right, and the cupola in front of Luna tops the Sea Beach Palace, which was the United States Government Building at the Centennial, and came to Coney to serve as the terminus of the New York & Sea Beach Railroad; the corresponding cupola across Surf Avenue housed Feltman's merry-go-round, and the coaster next to it is the Loop the Loop. Almost every structure that is neither restaurant nor roller coaster is a hotel.

SHORE LINE, EAST FROM DREAMLAND CHUTES. CONEY ISLAND.

We are back at the shore, and looking due east from the top of Dreamland's Shoot the Chutes. The long pier in the foreground is the Leapfrog Railway, an immensely elaborate device which sent two cars holding forty people each careering toward each other head-on; at the fatal moment of impact, one would scuttle harmlessly over the other's back. Beyond is the New Iron Pier: the speculators who built Dreamland absorbed the old one into their park. The substantial-looking tower to the left is part of an attraction called "New York to the North Pole"—Peary had reached the Pole in 1909, and people were interested in the Arctic—and far down the shore are the big frame hotels.

Pub. by I. Stern, Brooklyn, N. Y.   MANHATTAN BEACH HOTEL, MANHATTAN BEACH, N. Y.

During the season, every Coney Island resident with a couple of spare rooms to let called his house a hotel, but the greatest ones were grand by any standards. The first of these, the Manhattan Beach Hotel, was built in 1877. Designed by the architect J. Pickering Putnam, the hotel turned a front nearly seven hundred feet long toward the ocean, contained 258 rooms, and was surrounded by acres of nicely planted lawns and gardens. The kitchen could serve twenty thousand meals a day.

"One part of the pavilion," explained a guidebook published two years after the hotel opened, "is devoted to fish dinners, which are prepared by a special cook, and another part is reserved for the gratuitous use of the excursionists. . . . The hotel is furnished in all departments after the fashionable Eastlake style. The floors are of oiled woods, and there is no veneer or meretricious decoration."

Fresh water was piped in from the mainland; private detectives patrolled the beach; Gilmore's famous band gave open-air concerts every night. Best of all, the fashionable world had taken up the hotel: "The most exclusive and prominent clubs in New-York, the Union and the Union League, have selected it for a sea-beach branch, and have rented suites of the largest rooms permanently."

ON THE BOARD WALK (BRIGHTON) CONEY ISLAND, N.Y.

A rival to the Manhattan Beach Hotel opened its doors the next season: the Hotel Brighton, another vast Stick Style caravansary, could also feed twenty thousand people a day, put them up in perfect luxury, and—a feature the Manhattan Beach couldn't match—offer them champagne on draft at ten cents a glass. But try as it would, the Brighton never achieved quite the cachet of its eastern neighbor: it lay too near the amusement district of West Brighton to attract an entirely fashionable crowd.

Nevertheless, the Hotel Brighton was a splendid and prosperous establishment and it beat out the Manhattan Beach in one respect by being the object of a small work of technological genius. In 1888, with the sea washing away the shore from in front of the hotel, engineers raised the whole 6,000-ton structure onto 120 railway cars and inched it inland over newly laid track. The building started its ride on April 3, and was open for business on its new site by the end of June.

Bathing Crowd on a Hot Sunday Afternoon, Coney Island, N. Y.

30

It was the beach that had brought people to Coney in the beginning, and even with all the attractions that had grown up inland, they still came there to swim—or, more accurately, to wade. The flannel bathing suits of the day had to cover a good deal of skin, and the women's could weigh fifteen pounds wet. Many spent their day in the surf doggedly pulling themselves back and forth along ropes fixed to poles a hundred feet offshore, as they are doing here at Ward's Pavilion.

But even for those burdened down with pounds of sopping flannel, there was a bit of illicit freedom in splashing out into the ocean, and people felt the tang of it as soon as they stepped off the excursion boats. A writer named Elmer Blaney Harris, out to spend a Sunday at Coney, was making his way across the beach when he came upon "a little maid in wet, diaphanous green, combing her hair, her nether limbs part buried in the sand with which she had dried them."

Harris stopped and stared down at her—something he probably wouldn't have done to a girl on a park bench back in the everyday city. "My shadow fell upon her and she, with a question on her tongue, looked up as if . . . to demand by what right I obstructed her sunshine. I doffed my hat and apologized. She, smiling faintly, arched her head in ever so slight an inclination and went on with her combing. Her eyes were blue as the cloudless summer sky above us, the bath-dress she wore as translucent as sea-water when it leaps against the sun—a little image of jade and gold and ivory perched imperiously upon the sand. With regret I left her, wondering . . . whether chance would throw me in her way again."

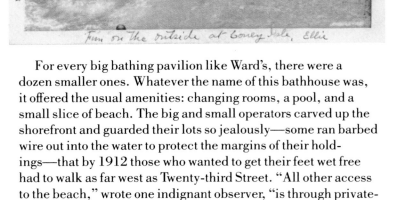

For every big bathing pavilion like Ward's, there were a dozen smaller ones. Whatever the name of this bathhouse was, it offered the usual amenities: changing rooms, a pool, and a small slice of beach. The big and small operators carved up the shorefront and guarded their lots so jealously—some ran barbed wire out into the water to protect the margins of their holdings—that by 1912 those who wanted to get their feet wet free had to walk as far west as Twenty-third Street. "All other access to the beach," wrote one indignant observer, "is through privately owned alleys leading to 'toll gate' hotels and pavilions."

However difficult it might be to find a patch of beach, nobody had any trouble getting to Surf Avenue, Coney's main street. Here, in between the entrances to the great parks, a hundred rides and shows stood side by side, fighting for their lives.

Only in the very early morning did Surf Avenue wear something of the aspect of the ordinary. Here is the street before the crowds come and, save for the crenellations of a scenic railway called the Rocky Road to Dublin, it looks pretty much like any turn-of-the-century commercial thoroughfare. The baker's wagon is delivering the day's supply of bread to the Sagamore Hotel's dining room, and behind it a brewer's much heavier wagon is bringing in hogsheads of beer—which always moved more briskly than bread on Coney. It will be a hot day, and all the hotel's awnings are put up against the sun.

Surf Avenue started to bustle as the morning wore on and the rides began to open. We are looking east toward the end of the amusement district. The observatory—called the Iron Tower and then, when the owners decided it would make customers feel better, the Steel Tower—rises above a ride whose advertising was cheeky even by Coney Island standards. The Great Musical Railway, which billed itself as "The Most Exciting Novelty and Greatest Ride on Earth," offered a trip across the continent— "scenic tunnels, great mechanical effects"—along with "Day & Night in the Alps," and, for good measure, a county fair. In fact, as one reporter was irritated to discover, there was no music at all, and the only scenery was a sign just before a terrifying drop which bore the superfluous injunction "No Kissing Allowed in This Tunnel."

The barnlike pavilion beyond is Camp's, where, beneath a placard with the brave message "21st Century Spectacular," ice cream was sold. "It is to Eat—It is to Laugh—It is to Drink," read the signs over the doors and running along the roof peak. The proprietors offered a $1,000 reward "for proof of any adulteration found in our sherbets."

Surf Avenue, Coney Island, N. Y.

By midafternoon with a fair-sized crowd, Surf Avenue looked like this. Some wealthy types are venturing over from Manhattan Beach in their motor cars; or they may just be wage earners out in a taxi—fifty cents for the first half-mile, ten cents for each additional quarter mile. " 'Tis a true thing they say that Coney levels all rank," one of O. Henry's people says. "I see millionaires eatin' popcorn and trampin' along with the crowd; and I see eight-dollar-a-week clothin'-store clerks in red automobiles fightin' one another for who'd squeeze the horn when they come to a corner."

Surf Avenue ran wide open until about two in the morning. This nighttime view was probably photographed during the day and transformed by the printer, but the cool dazzle of the lights and the low, purple sky are accurate enough.

The big parks generated their own electricity, but the lighting on the small attractions was sufficiently spectacular for the Edison Company to want full credit. The Electric Scenic Railway belongs to LaMarcus A. Thompson, who deserved his profitable chunk of street frontage, for he is the father of the roller coaster.

For all its noise and crowds, Surf Avenue was stately in comparison with the Bowery. A short, narrow walk that ran between Steeplechase Park and Feltman's restaurant, the Bowery was the clangorous distillate of Coney Island. It looks tranquil in this scene taken very early in the day and in the century, but as soon as it got dark the Silver Dollar Hotel would, like all its neighbors, generate an immense amount of music, smoke, and shouting, while the establishment across the way pushed staggering numbers of five-cent beers across its counter.

Elmer Blaney Harris made his way down a short stretch of the Bowery: " . . . only two blocks . . . but they were busy blocks—eating booths, hot frankfurters on the grill, beef dripping on the spit, wash-boilers of green corn steaming in the center of hungry groups who gnawed the ears as if playing harmonicas; photograph galleries, the sitters ghastly in the charnel-house glare . . . chop suey joints, fez-topped palmists, strength-tests; dance halls and continuous song-and-dance entertainments, the girls in white, according to the regulation that obliges them to lay off their tights and spangles out of respect for the Sabbath. Bands, orchestras, pianos, at war with gramophones, hand-organs, calliopes; overhead, a roar of wheels in a deathlock with shrieks and screams; whistles, gongs, rifles all busy; the smell of candy, popcorn, meats, beer, tobacco, blended with the odor of the crowd redolent now and then of patchouli; a streaming river of people arched over by electric signs— this is the Bowery at Coney Island."

On the Bowery, Coney Island, N. Y.

Every spring the newspapers would send their men out to Coney, and they always came back with the same story: last year the place had been a lair of petty grifters and tainted food, this year it was a civic paradise. There was more conviction to these stories after the parks went up, but the Bowery always resisted benign interpretation.

O. Henry seemed skeptical of a Bowery renaissance; in any event, his character Dennis Carnahan, down for the day to cheer himself after quarreling with his girl at the Dairymen and Street-Sprinkler Drivers' semiannual ball, was unconvinced: "Ye will have heard that Coney has received moral reconstruction. The old Bowery, where they used to take your tintype by force and give ye knockout drops before having your palm read, is now called the Wall Street of the island. The wienerwurst stands are required by law to keep a news ticker in 'em; and the dough-nuts are examined every four years by a retired steamboat in-spector. The reprehensible and degradin' resorts that disgraced old Coney are said to be wiped out. The wipin'-out process consists of raisin' the price from 10 cents to 25 cents, and hirin' a blonde named Maudie to sell tickets instead of Micky, the Bowery Bite. That's what they say—I don't know."

The roller coaster is the aristocrat of park attractions, and Coney always had several in operation. Here, one of the larger ones carries a trainload of grave-looking passengers skyward before flinging them into the drop.

America's first coaster was built on Coney, and they went through every stage of their evolution there. LaMarcus A. Thompson came from Chicago in 1884 to put up what he called his Switchback Railway, which was nothing more than two parallel stretches of track six hundred feet long. A car holding ten people rolled gently down to the end of the first track and was hoisted to the second while the passengers filed up a stairway to a platform where car and riders were reunited, and rolled back to the starting point. This mild creation cost its inventor $1,600 to build. It took in over $500 a day.

Almost immediately a man named Alcoke saw how much time and effort could be saved if the track ends were joined in a loop. He got his ride working before the season was over: it was, said a reporter, "a contrivance designed to give the passengers, for the insignificant expenditure of five cents, all the sensation of being carried away by a cyclone." Next year, Philip Hinckle built a coaster that drew its cars up with a moving chain—the system still in use today.

Blandly called a "centrifugal pleasure railway," the ghastly Flip-Flap gave the necks of its passengers a vicious tug on every ride. It appeared almost as soon as the standard roller coaster had been worked out, and it tortured passengers for a season or two at Boyton's Sea Lion Park. When word got around that the device really *did* hurt, it went out of business.

LOOPING THE LOOP.   CONEY ISLAND

LOOP THE L

Eventually engineers figured out what was wrong with the Flip-Flap. It was not that it went upside down, but that the twenty-five-foot loop was perfectly circular. An ellipse, it seemed, gentled the action of the ride enough to keep it from damaging passengers.

Edward Prescott designed his ride carefully, built it on West Tenth Street, and called it the Loop the Loop. Sturdily braced and made entirely of steel, it fulfilled the oxymoronic requirements of any successful roller coaster: it must seem at once totally lethal and absolutely safe.

The machine appeared solid enough to seduce the writer Albert Bigelow Paine, who initially had "declared strenuously against this appalling device," into giving it a try. "A fierce upward rush of air, a wild grip at a loosening hat, and an instant later the shock. We were on the loop. We were shooting upward as a billow that breaks against the cliff; we were curling over as the wave curls backward; we were darting down to inevitable annihilation! . . . For what seemed an eternal instant we were hanging in mid-air. . . my body was swaying in a well-defined centrifugal impulse to close up like an accordion. Then all at once we had dropped, and were shooting outward, dazed, weak and wondering at our safety. . . . An unknown man in the back seat announced that he would not do it again for a thousand dollars. The figures did not seem extravagant."

The ride looked almost that scary from the ground, and people paid admission just to watch. But the cars could carry only four passengers in five minutes; a regular coaster could carry twenty-four in half the time, and those figures doomed the Loop the Loop.

Showmen were always seeking a successful roller coaster variant, and most of their inventions first saw the light of day out at Coney. The island was known as the Gibraltar of the amusement world; there was really no other place for the committed entrepreneur to test a ride. If it could survive on Coney, it was sure to go in Omaha.

And so the Whirl-Fly came to the island to try its fortunes under its singularly unappealing emblem—although the device was nowhere near so grand as the juggernaut pictured in this lithograph. Changing the name to the more musical Whirlifly was not sufficient to save the ride.

PIKES PEAK RAILWAY

40

L. A. Thompson responded to the competition by developing the scenic railway, a roller coaster that rattled through dark tunnels where tableaux of enchanted grottoes and alpine scenes and the like lit up as the cars approached.

Thompson's first scenic railway did so well that before long he built his second one a few hundred yards west of it on Surf Avenue. This quiet scene—with the empty electric tour bus in the foreground—belies the scenic railway's considerable success. One witness was amused that where once "the ride alone sufficed," now scenery was required. "Across the park is Switzerland with chalets, frozen torrents, and the alpen glow, the cars

sleigh-shaped and laden with bells; elsewhere . . . are . . . scenes from a mining camp, showing picturesque wax figures at work over derrick or cradle by the side of a running stream; a ride through the Dragon's Gorge in Luna Park shows you the Arctic Regions, the Bottom of the Sea, and other familiar pictures from dime geography."

By 1909, L. A. Thompson was running a company capitalized at $900,000 supplying coasters to parks across the country for prices that reached as high as $100,000, and enjoying the steady exchange of lawsuits with rival manufacturers that was a staple of the outdoor amusement industry.

TOURING THE ALPS *Coney Island*

The new century's faith in its burgeoning technology is nowhere better demonstrated than in this coaster, which drew its power from a third rail and was run by a motorman. A number of these absurdly labor-intensive devices went up at Coney. On a busy day there would be three or four trains, each with its own motorman, running on one coaster, carefully regulated by electric block signals that shone red and green. So a coaster owner might find himself operating an honest-to-God little railroad.

Having an engineer in charge of the train did nothing to take the edge off the ride. Elmer Blaney Harris wrote of this one, "We swung free of the cliffs and faced the lights of the park and the straight, narrow parallel drop of the tracks, sagging like tight-ropes. In the cañons below, cars seemed to be shooting in all directions, in and out of tunnels and around sharp curves or over trestles. We braced ourselves, and our little dwarf of a train shot over. A prolonged, lifting cry broke from the women in the seats in front of us, a cry not of fear, not of joy, not of pain; a cry peculiar, even uncanny, having all of these things blended with something delicious and startling—the Coney Island cry!"

This is the entrance to the "Rough Riders" on the Bowery.

These are some of the Hills you go over on the "Rough Riders" at Coney Island

The Rough Riders, another third-rail coaster, was run by attendants wearing Spanish-American War uniforms, and the trains carried customers past tableaux of that brief contest before crackling up the first steep grade. Despite the "sense of security [given] by the presence of an attendant," said *Scientific American*, "rides which have motor auxiliaries are not any safer than the gravity ride." A coaster motorman named E. J. Quinby remembered his boss explaining just how he wanted the ride run: "Listen for the screams. You can always tell how you're doin' by how loud they holler. If you want to keep your job here, ya gotta make 'em yell bloody murder."

Quinby made them holler. So did the other motormen. "On the steep downgrades these rascals were instructed to coast, but they invariably used full power. . . . The subsequent sharp curve was accordingly entered at such speed that the whole structure would creak and groan under the strain. . . ." In 1910 a Rough Riders motorman took his train through the curves so violently that two cars tore loose and pitched sixteen people into thin air sixty feet above Surf Avenue. Four of them died.

By the end of the first decade of the century, the roller coaster had clattered into its maturity. Banked turns had been found to give a smoother ride, and then modified because couples didn't want it to be that smooth; operators had learned that the trains actually ran faster on hot days because the grease packing in the wheels liquefied; a series of violent little bumps had been added to give a final fillip at the ride's end, and abandoned as excessive; and the Loop the Loop was going into an eclipse that would last for seventy years.

The result was a series of machines on the order of the Giant Racer, a pow-erful modern double-tracked steel coaster which carried two trainloads of people through its great racketing arcs side by side. It—and the coasters like it—offered some of the island's fiercest pleasures, not only in the brutal plunges, but in the windy hush of the climb that preceded them: "The climbing chain grates, grips the cogs," wrote John Dos Passos of a Coney Island roller coaster, "jerkily the car climbs the incline out of the whirring lights, out of the smell of crowds and steamed corn and peanuts, up jerkily grating up through the tall night of Sep-tember meteors."

44

Lots of attractions on Coney imitated things—the Doge's Palace, Pike's Peak, a submarine voyage—but nothing was as grimly literal as the Great Deep Rift Coal Mine. The owners did run a frill of light bulbs along the eaves and put a shooting gallery in the company store instead of shovels and nails and kerosene, but otherwise this structure was identical to a thousand others in the Pennsylvania coalfields. Unglamorous though it was, the fuel for America's industrial muscle was coming out of haggard barns like this one, and it drew respectful crowds. "Although not a real mine," one guidebook explained, "the illusion is so perfect that the trip affords an instructive as well as pleasurable treat."

Henry J. Pain came to Coney Island from England in the 1880s to "inaugurate a series of pyrotechnic displays of the grandest character, far excelling any ever given in America, or indeed at the Crystal and Alexandra Palaces, London." He did so well with his "Wonderful Triumphs of Science and Art" that he stayed on season after season, at first operating on Manhattan Beach, and then opening this handsomely planted grandstand on Brighton Beach.

Many of Pain's shows had rudimentary plots. In this one, spectators sitting on a creaking infinity of bentwood chairs saw scores of people in togas running back and forth while Mount Vesuvius spewed out colored fire and Pompeii disappeared beneath torrents of blazing magnesium powder. The program would change if a good world crisis came along: Pain also subjected the Spanish Fleet and the Russian defenses at Vladivostok to his gorgeous annihilation.

View of Pain's Fire Works, Manhattan Beach, N.Y.

Nothing stirred a showman more than a truly devastating catastrophe. Not long after a tidal wave swept across Galveston, Texas, and killed some seven thousand people, New Yorkers could see the Gulf city washed away in an intricately staged spectacular that used real water, fake water, scrims, and hundreds of model buildings.

At the time this card was made, Coney had three equally ambitious disasters running simultaneously on Surf Avenue. The proprietors of the Galveston Flood offered those spectators who wanted more

carnage a free bus ride to the Johnstown Flood. The owners kept abreast of the latest cataclysms: when, for instance, an earthquake devastated Messina in 1908, the Johnstown Flood became the Great Italian Earthquake.

The producers of the Mont Pelée spectacle assured patrons that the 1,200-seat auditorium "is provided with eleven exits, and may be emptied in two minutes." One reporter commented tartly that the public's "delight for horrors" remained strong, "only the public must be guaranteed absolute personal safety."

CARTER & GUT, PUBLISHERS, N. Y.

SCENE FROM THE STUPENDOUS REPRODUCTION OF THE GREAT TIDAL WAVE

THE GALVESTON FLOOD

AT CONEY ISLAND, OPPOSITE CULVER DEPOT

SHOWING A SMALL PORTION OF THE IMMENSE SCENE OF THE CITY OF GALVESTON, BEFORE THE FLOOD

CARTER & GUT, PUBLISHERS, N. Y.

SCENE FROM THE STUPENDOUS REPRODUCTION OF THE GREAT TIDAL WAVE

THE GALVESTON FLOOD

AT CONEY ISLAND, OPPOSITE CULVER DEPOT

SHOWING A SMALL PORTION OF THE IMMENSE SCENE OF THE CITY OF GALVESTON, AFTER THE FLOOD

GENERAL P. A. CRONJE

THE STUPENDOUS BOER WAR SPECTACLE NOW AT
BRIGHTON BEACH PARK

SURFACE AND ELEVATED CARS LEAVE BROOKLYN BRIDGE EVERY MINUTE

48

"Twenty years ago," said Frederic Thompson, who had a hand in a number of staged spectaculars before he built Luna Park, "the cyclorama, showing the Gettysburg battlefield with the dead, the wounded, the fighters and the clouds, all still, was very well, and attracted great numbers of spectators, but it would not do now. Now the clouds must move, the men must be living, the whole scene must be full of action . . . and the showman who gets the greatest amount of action into his scenes is the one who stands most chance of pleasing the crowds."

It was this demand that brought General Piet Cronje to Coney Island—surely the last place on earth the old Boer warrior would have expected to end his career. He had fought so ably against the British in South Africa that he was one of the most famous military men in the world by February of 1900, when he surrendered his five thousand weary burghers to Lord Roberts' overwhelming force at the Modder River in the Orange Free State.

With the war over, a Missouri-born entrepreneur named Alfred W. Lewis convinced a number of British and Boer veterans to come across the Atlantic and refight it for the St. Louis World's Fair. Lewis' greatest coup was getting Cronje to join his paramilitary force.

The Boer War show did so well in St. Louis that William Aloysius Brady decided he wanted it. The quintessential New York showman of the era, Brady was equally at home staging Shakespeare and managing Jim Corbett in his epochal fight with John L. Sullivan. He kept track of the show during its increasingly rocky post-fair tour, and when it finally went broke in a Southern tank town, Brady wired enough money to bring the two armies to Coney Island.

On a patch of swampland between the Brighton Beach and Manhattan Beach hotels, Brady set a thousand men to work. Through the first chilly months of 1905 they hammered together a grandstand that could seat twelve thousand people, while fifty-eight artists painted hundreds of yards of canvas and metalsmiths soldered together great zinc troughs which, pumped full of water, would become the Modder River.

The actors arrived early in the spring, straight up from the south in boxcars, twenty men to a car. "They were," said Brady, "the sorriest-looking crew in Christendom . . . chilly, starved, dismal—and fighting mad." They had a neat military camp set up for them, and they were able to get clean in the frigid ocean. They were also able to get drunk in the Brighton Beach Hotel, and Brady had to kick "an ugly, shambling Boer with a loud mouth" in the solar plexus before he could establish his authority. After that, the men saluted him, and things went smoothly.

CARTER & OUT, PUBLISHERS, N.Y.

DE WET'S ESCAPE

THE STUPENDOUS BOER WAR SPECTACLE NOW AT
BRIGHTON BEACH PARK
SURFACE AND ELEVATED CARS LEAVE BROOKLYN BRIDGE EVERY MINUTE

Brady beefed his 600-man force up with locals until he was able to field a thousand troops on opening day. The show began with a few British scouts riding into an ambush, and promptly burst into a full-scale battle, with cannon roaring away hub to hub, battalions of riflemen firing blanks in each other's faces, and General Christiaan de Wet (but not the real one) recreating the pell-mell escape that had saved his life the one time the British caught the great cavalryman napping.

The only problem was that the big guns made the horses at the nearby Brighton Beach racetrack skittish, and so at post time the thundering veldt would fall eerily silent for a minute. This interruption notwithstanding, the Boer War pageant was a success from the start: "It's a good show," wrote the *New York Times* critic, "a big show, and one that makes the red blood tingle and sends the thrills of patriotic fervor up and down the spine."

What do you think of that N. L.

These African tribesmen were brought along to add a touch of realism to the show, but mostly to do heavy work around the camp and take care of the stock. They were promised $4 a week, and given nothing. After all, the promoters reasoned, what could they do about it once they were six thousand miles from home?

But as it turned out, the New World's democratic air infected them, and shortly after they got to St. Louis, the Africans went on strike. On May 6, 1904, said the *St. Louis Republican*, "the half-clad blacks rushed to a lumber pile and raised sticks which they brandished like their native war spears, at the same time hurling words of defiance at British and Boers." The sometime enemies overcame their differences for long enough to put down the rebellion.

The next month, however, fifteen blacks fled the show. This time the press, which had been jocose about the first quarrel, was sympathetic: the defection was reported as a "break for liberty." The Negro community of St. Louis rose in defense of the refugees, and the police captured them only after a fight.

Sergeant O'Leary returned the natives to the fair, but before the show was over, some twenty Africans managed to disappear into America.

T he show, of course, had to end with General Cronje surrendering to a surrogate Lord Roberts, but before that the Boers got in their licks.

At St. Louis, Cronje had been forced to meet the crowds after after each show, but he was spared that humiliation at Coney. Brady built him a cottage behind the grandstand, and at the end of the day the old Boer sat on the porch with his wife, smoking his pipe in the riotous Coney Island evening.

Despite its success, the show did not make enough money to cover the soldiers' salaries, and sometime in August they began to drift away. Brady managed to keep enough troops on hand to stay open through Labor Day, but that was that. There was no Boer War Spectacle the next summer.

Many of the actors went back to fighting real wars; there was always something martial going on in South America, and mercenaries were in demand. "I'll bet," said Brady years later, "there are little Latin-looking girls and boys in Guatemala and San Salvador today whose names are Smith and Dykgraaf because their papas were hornswoggled into coming over to fight the Boer War for the delectation of the St. Louis World's Fair."

A CLOSING SCENE OF THE BATTLE OF COLENSO

THE STUPENDOUS BOER WAR SPECTACLE NOW AT BRIGHTON BEACH PARK

SURFACE AND ELEVATED CARS LEAVE BROOKLYN BRIDGE EVERY MINUTE

8171. GOAT CARRIAGES, CONEY ISLAND, N. Y.   COPYRIGHT, 1904, BY DETROIT PHOTOGRAPHIC CO.

Not every attraction on Coney required the participation of European armies or doomed cities. There were thousands of lesser diversions: shooting galleries, ring-toss booths, weight-guessers, wheels of fortune—and goat carts. Year after year, while the grand spectacles came and went, children continued to love being pulled along in a neat little carriage by a billy goat.

CHIRA PAGODA

BRIGHTON BEACH, C. I.

"We went into an enchanted chicken coop," said O. Henry, "which was fixed mysterious with red cloth and pictures of hands with lines crossing 'em like a railroad centre. The sign over the door says it is Madame Zozo the Egyptian Palmist." Madame Zozo revealed that "the line of your fate shows . . . that ye've not arrived at your time of life without bad luck. . . . Ye'll make a voyage upon the water very soon, and have a financial loss. I see one line that brings good luck. There's a man coming into your life who will fetch ye good fortune. . . ."

Although Chira's rather tonish establishment suggests his delivery may have been more polished, all palmists had pretty much the same line of chatter. But Richard Le Gallienne dismissed this sort of cheap omniscience, declaring that you have no business going to Coney Island "if you are too superior to have your fortune told by some peasant woman who knows nothing about it, and knows you know she doesn't."

However elaborate the shows and scenic railways that flourished there, at least half Coney Island's lure was always food, and nobody served up a better shore dinner than Charles Feltman.

Feltman started out offering far humbler fare than the noble heap of seafood shown in this lithograph, but at the beginning of his career he made a contribution to American life that will last as long as the Republic itself.

Charles Feltman invented the hot dog.

Of course, this claim is disputed. But those who favor Feltman can bulwark their case with a reassuring amount of detail. As a young German immigrant, Feltman drove a pie wagon up and down the beach at Coney, and by 1867 (or 1874; accounts vary) he had a good business going for himself. But there was a problem: his customers were asking for hot sandwiches. This would mean a lot of carving and slicing and paraphernalia, and Feltman resisted it. Then one day he had an idea.

He went to a wheelwright named Donovan and asked if it would be possible to fix up a stove in the pie wagon. If so, Feltman could keep a supply of hot sausages on hand and simply fork them onto split milk rolls whenever anybody wanted a hot sandwich. Donovan said it was no problem, and installed the stove on the spot. Feltman set some sausages on to boil and in a little while, there in Donovan's shop on East New York and Howard Avenues in Brooklyn, the two men ate the world's first two hot dogs.

FELTMANS, CONEY ISLAND, N.Y.

FELTMANS

Feltman parlayed his hot dog into this verdant fiefdom, which ran along West Tenth Street from Surf Avenue to the shore. He stocked his Deutscher Garden with the favorite diversions of his German boyhood—bands in lederhosen, beer in fine big schooners, mottoes urging his customers not to argue. To this ancient recreational mixture he added such New World ingredients as the Ziz, a roller coaster that surged back and forth through the trees.

FELTMANS' Upper Veranda Service the Shore Dinner De Luxe CONEY ISLAND

Here on this breezeway, and in a growing labyrinth of gardens and restaurants below, as many as twelve hundred waiters could serve up eight thousand meals at a time. Despite this terrific press of business, Feltman's remained one of the pleasantest places on the island, and people loved to sit and drink beer under the leafy boughs of the maple trees.

It was here that Elmer Blaney Harris found the girl he had seen on the beach, "the maid of the golden hair and sea-green bathing suit. She was sitting alone, entirely preoccupied with eating a bit of sandwich, and I had ample time to note the faded roses on her last year's hat and the characteristic grace of her hands before she looked up and saw me. . . .

"I caught Dora's eye (her name was Dora, if I may announce it without being anti-climactic) and in the freemasonry of the crowd we laughed simultaneously. At her table was the only unoccupied chair in the garden, and I asked if I might sit there.

" 'Sure, you can sit there!' said she, still smiling. 'Anyone can sit here with a laugh like that. I'm never afraid of a man if he laughs loud.'

" 'Are you alone?'

" 'Of course I'm alone! . . . Oh, you needn't think I'm alone because I have to be, or because I like it. I s'pose there's thousands of men in this crowd I'd like, but—well, most of 'em—you know how it is—always the third rail—see?'

"I told her I saw perfectly, and that, if she pleased, we'd walk between the tracks."

Thus were friendships formed on Coney in the summer.

FELTMANS' SEASIDE GARDEN Superb Motion Pictures CONEY ISLAND

When motion pictures came in, Feltman added them to his repertory of diversions—and so, it seemed, did half the other entrepreneurs on the island.

Movies had been good business on Coney since 1895, when a four-minute epic showing a round between Young Griffo and Battling Charles Barnett enjoyed a successful season's run under a tent on Surf Avenue.

In the summer of 1910, *Scientific American* said there were over 450 different motion pictures playing simultaneously. The figure seems phenomenal, but crowds who shunned the stifling Manhattan theaters were happy to sit outdoors even if the screen was somewhat dimmed by the surrounding glare. The theaters were designed to catch every possible breath of air: "Open-faced moving-picture shows," said an observer, ran "with shades dropped so that passersby could not steal a glimpse without stooping down, which ignoble attitude never failed to invite effrontery from the jocose crowd."

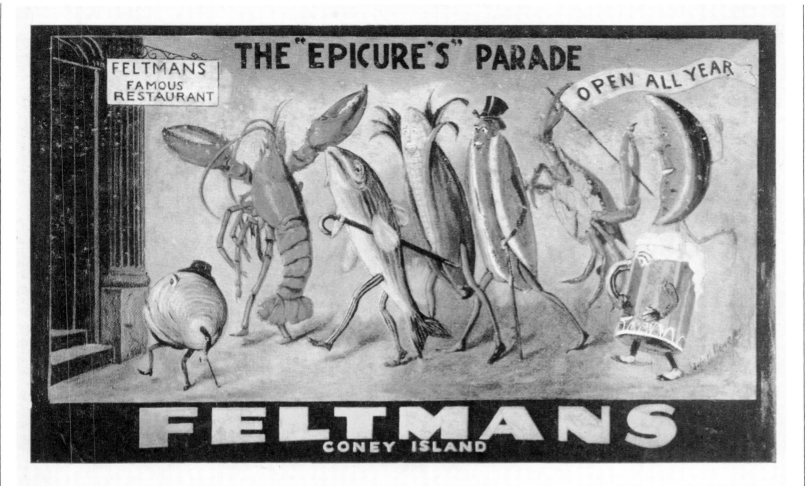

Along with his movie theater, Feltman installed a dance hall, his roller coaster, and a series of carousels until his restaurant had all the elements of an independent amusement park.

But it was the food and drink that kept bringing customers back, just as it had in the beginning. During the 1880s, Feltman served 200,000 people a season, and nearly twice that many during the 1890s. By the first decade of this century the number of customers had risen to 900,000 a year; by the second, 2,000,000. They ate clams and lobsters, clams and crabs, clams and steak—but although the hot dog is toward the rear of this parade, it was never abandoned: scattered throughout Feltman's huge restaurant, seven grills kept busy turning them out.

When he died in 1910, the sometime pieman passed on to his two sons a business worth more than $1,000,000.

If Feltman's was a place of bowers and gardens, Stauch's was pure urban swank. Louis Stauch, a sharp, slight, nervous man who dressed like a country deacon, came to Coney as a teenager in the mid-1870s and got a job playing piano beneath the oil lamps in a saloon. In a few years he had taken over the place, and before long he owned a valuable slice of land stretching from the Bowery to the ocean. Here he built this impressive restaurant and dance hall, which looks as substantial as any big-city railroad terminal.

Stauch's, Coney Island, N. Y.

Grill Room, Stauch's, Coney Island, New York.

Stauch's place was solid, comfortable, and roomy—which was just as well, because he never left it. When he took his first job on the island, his employer is said to have asked him, "If I give you a regular job, will you stick?" Stauch said he'd stick, and he did. He ate in his restaurant, was measured for his clothes in his restaurant, and slept in his restaurant. In a quarter century, he never spent a single night away from Coney.

Stauch said his ballroom had the largest dance floor in the world, and whether or not this is true, it was an impressive operation. Three thousand couples could get out there at once, and do the Grizzly Bear to Al Ferguson's band.

Stauch, that most careful of managers, would have hated Elmer Blaney Harris' assessment of his ballroom.

Harris had made Dora the proposition "What do you say to showing me around the Island?" Early in the tour, "We took a peek in at Stauch's dance hall. The place reeked of beer, and above the oblong of dancers, some *gauche*, some graceful, all cheek to cheek, very business-like, hung a cloud of cigarette smoke. The small tables beyond the railing were deserted during the dance, but filled as the music ended after a perfunctory encore, and waiters, sweat-marked and sullen, began the harvest that supports the place, counting their tips between whiles as a dog guards a bone."

Ball Room and Balcony, Dining Room, Stauch's, Coney Island, N. Y.

Cigar Department in Lobby of Stauch's, Coney Island, New York.

Something of the fierce and somber attention Stauch paid to every aspect of his business can be seen in this immaculate cigar stand, the equal of anything in Manhattan. Day and night he prowled through his restaurant, going upstairs to bed for a while when he got sleepy, then returning to his endless rounds, checking the glasses in his four bars, making sure the dance floor was sufficiently glossy.

Friends told him to take a vacation; he shook his head: "People gad about too much."

When, late in his life, he finally married, he spent his honeymoon at Stauch's.

HENDERSON'S
CONEY ISLAND.

OPEN ALL YEAR

RESTAURANT
MUSIC HALL

Fred Henderson offered the crowds still further acreage of
food in the tall, wide reaches of his main dining room.
Henderson came to Coney Island early, and was well established
as a restaurateur by the 1880s. When one of the many fires that
regularly leveled the Bowery without managing to change its
character destroyed his frame restaurant, Henderson replaced it
with a brick one, and threw in a music hall.

HENDERSON'S MUSIC HALL – CONEY ISLAND

Henderson staged shows on a Broadway scale, having taken to heart an inadvertent lesson in theatrical economics. He was out West when his son telegraphed to say that the music hall's comic opera company was doing poorly. Deciding to cut his losses, Henderson wired back, "Put in another company." The son misunderstood, and simply added a new troupe to the one already there. The overhead should have brought on immediate bankruptcy; instead, Henderson came back to find his crowded stage playing to crowded houses, and turning a good profit. Coney Island audiences tended to make extravagance pay handsomely.

RUMFORD PRESS, CONCORD, N. H.

BOWERY ENTRANCE.
Geo. C. Tilyou's Beautiful Steeplechase Park, Coney Island N. Y.

Having a grand time Sallie

66

For decades the Steeplechase Man was as familiar to millions of Americans as the Indian on the penny. That terrible face with its hair falling away from the part in two sculpted fillips and its death-rictus grin glared out over summer crowds for nearly seventy years. Many hated it—one critic called it "the most incredibly vulgar" trademark he had ever seen—but it so perfectly reflected the mechanical fun generated in Steeplechase that people came to believe it actually was the portrait of George C. Tilyou, the park's creator.

It wasn't. Tilyou had a long, grave, aristocrat's face; but the Steeplechase Man was emblematic of Tilyou's particular genius: once people put themselves in his hands he could get them laughing and keep them laughing. The factory he built on Surf Avenue kept turning out laughing people long after Tilyou was gone, long after the other Coney Island parks were gone.

Tilyou opened Steeplechase Park in 1897 on fifteen acres of land between Surf Avenue and the ocean. It was touch and go for a while—on busy days he is said to have dragged in furniture from his home to give the crowds extra seating—but by 1901 he could write, "This stupendous amusement forms the most enchanting and magnetic fun-making resort in the world."

In 1907 it burned down. The next morning Tilyou put up a sign "To Inquiring Friends":

> I have trouble today that I did not have yesterday.
> I had troubles yesterday that I have not today.
> On this site will be erected shortly a better,
>   bigger, greater Steeplechase Park.
> Admission to the Burning Ruins — 10 Cents.

During the months that followed, a great glass-and-cast-iron shed rose from the rubble. This was Tilyou's Pavilion of Fun, and it gave him an advantage over every other amusement park man in the country—the rides were indoors. Tilyou was a devout man. He went to church every Sunday. His rivals said he was praying for rain.

67

Steeple Chase,
Coney Island, N. Y.

The park's main attraction was not indoors; it girdled the Pavilion of Fun. "The Gravity Steeplechase Race Course," said a 1900 promotion brochure, is "one of the biggest winners ever known, both in profit and in popularity. It combines the fun of the merry-go-round, the excitement of the chutes, and adds to the charm of both the zest of a genuine race, appealing to the sporting blood. . . . A ride on the horses is a healthful stimulant that stirs the heart and clears the brain. It straightens out wrinkles and irons out puckers; cares and worries are forgotten; the dashing pleasure of the moment is all in all."

Tilyou's motto, "Half a mile in half a minute, and fun all the time," was preposterous—the ride didn't go anything like sixty miles an hour—but it really did simulate a horserace. "The tracks being parallel and the starting and finishing points adjacent, you can start a horse on each track at the same time, and as . . . the rider . . . can accelerate or diminish its speed by the manner in which he handles it on the ascending and descending grades . . . an actual race can be run. All the main features of regular courses are provided, such as judges' stand, finish wire, half and quarter-mile post, badges, bugler, attendants dressed as jockeys, etc."

Here, the horses are being pulled eight abreast to the starting gate.

A couple hundred feet from the gate, horses and riders rock toward the first turn. As the gentle slopes suggest, the ride was not much of a thriller. The author Rupert Hughes, who is certainly the only man ever to invoke Tennyson in criticizing an amusement park, spoke of "the steeplechase, where men and women straddle the same hobby-horse and slide yelling down the ringing grooves of small change."

Hughes missed the point. The roller coasters were scarier, the tunnels of love more secluded, and yet nothing on Coney gave quite the same sense of jaunty intimacy as sitting astride that horse, the man behind the woman, arms around her waist holding the reins, and gusting along through the summer evening.

During the park's third season, a million people rode the Steeplechase, and the numbers grew with the new century.

INTERIOR VIEW
STEEPLECHASE PARK,
CONEY ISLAND, N.Y.

70

The lofty roof of the Pavilion of Fun covered more than five acres of hardwood floor, where Tilyou's rides shook and spun. During the park's first few seasons, its owner liked to advertise that he "is the inventor of all the amusement novelties in his big plant," and although that changed by the time the Pavilion went up, Steeplechase prospered solely through Tilyou's understanding of how people worked.

The steeplechase ride cost $37,000 to build; the park's second "big hit," Tilyou said, "cost me precisely $5."

"I built a flight of six steps up to a table, placed a box on this and in the box put three broken bricks." He advertised this exhibit as "The California Red Bats." "Then I charged ten cents a look." People climbed the ladder, peered into the box, found they were looking at *brick*bats, climbed back down, and refused—as Tilyou had known they would—to say what they'd seen. "Naturally the curiosity spread like the measles and in that season 300,000 people came to see [that] exhibit."

August 16-1914

COMBINATION TICKET GUIDE

Steeplechase
CONEY ISLAND'S
Only Funny Place

WHERE 25,000 PEOPLE LAUGH AT ONE TIME

GEO. C. TILYOU'S NEW STEEPLECHASE PARK
Pavilion of Fun

Get the Famous Combination Ticket of Admission and

25 BIG ATTRACTIONS 25c

The Place of the "Great Michelin Twins"

HERE THEY ARE

1—BARREL OF FUN	. . . . .	Bowery Entrance
2—TRAVELER	. . . .	Surf Avenue Entrance
3—THE MIXER	. . . .	Bowery Entrance
4—VENETIAN GONDOLAS	. . .	Surf Avenue Front
5—CHANTICLEER	. . . .	"
6—GOLDEN STAIRS	. . . .	Pavilion of Fun
7—BOUNDING BILLOWS	. . . .	" "
8—WHIRLPOOL	. . . .	" "
9—ROOF GARDEN	. . . .	" "
10—RAZZLE DAZZLE	. . . .	" "
11—HUMAN ROULETTE	. . . .	" "
12—BICYCLES	. . . .	" "
13—CAVE OF WINDS	. . . .	" "
14—SOUTH POLE	. . . .	" "
15—SOUP BOWL	. . . .	" "
16—SCHOOL DAYS OR BARREL OF LOVE		" "
17—FERRIS WHEEL	. . . .	Sunken Gardens
18—MOVING PICTURES	. . . .	" "
19—GLASS WORKS	. . . .	
20—ROLLER COASTER	. . . .	Ocean Pier
21—PIER TROLLEY	. . . .	
22—UNCLE SAM	. . . .	Pavilion of Fun
23—HUMAN POOL TABLE	. . .	
24—AIR SHIPS	. . . .	Sunken Gardens
25—DOWN AND OUT	. . . .	Pavilion of Fun

FREE *100 Additional Attractions* FREE

Beautiful Gardens — Swell Bathing Beach — Superb Swimming Pool
King of all Amusements — Steeplechase Race Course

ALL IRON STEAMBOATS LAND AT STEEPLECHASE PIER

Tilyou once told a reporter, "I would say that any success in the amusement business is unaccountable." In fact, he knew exactly where his lay: in the knowledge that people would happily put up with a few minutes of humiliation if they could in turn watch others being humiliated. To this end patches of floor heaved, air jets sent skirts and petticoats foaming up around ankles, chairs dispensed electric shocks, and staircases flattened into slides: "The Funny Stairway," said Tilyou's promotion, "has . . . caused laughter enough to cure all the dyspepsia in the world. The ladder of fame is not in it with the funny stairway."

By the time this menu of diversions had been compiled, the Roof Garden had joined the list. A sign above an elevator directed customers to the lovely roof garden; the car would appear, the operator would let people in, close the gates, and tug on a rope, and with a tremendous crash the car would slam backward to lie wrecked at a forty-five-degree angle while the panicked occupants scrambled for safety. The floor was oiled, however, and few made it until the fake car was righted. *Scientific American*, in one of its annual discussions of what was new out at Coney, dutifully described this device, then commented, "Truly a little thing amuses some people."

GEO. C. TILYOU'S STEEPLECHASE - FUNNY PLACE - HOOP-LA.

This simple machine was one of Til-you's most reliable crowd-pleasers. He first built it before there was a Steeplechase and called it the Razzle Dazzle. After a while it became known as the Wedding Ring. When this card was posted in 1915 it was called the Hoopla, but it was still the same medieval mechanism. Up to seventy people crowded onto a six-ton circle of laminated wood, and clung there yelling while attendants underneath pushed it back and forth. Tilyou once tried to modernize it by hooking up an engine, but people preferred the erratic motion imparted by human muscle. This picture is somewhat confusing because, in an attempt to be helpful, the postcard manufacturer had planking painted in over the pit where the operators labored.

HUMAN ROULETTE WHEEL, STEEPLECHASE, THE FUNNY PLACE, CONEY ISLAND, N. Y.

Tilyou got the idea for the Human Roulette Wheel during a walk along the beach, when he came upon some children spinning each other on the wheel of an abandoned overturned cart. He devised this huge, polished wooden disc which spun people off it and, like another Tilyou invention, the Barrel of Love, allowed couples to do some satisfactory tumbling around in each other's arms.

This grim team is putatively enjoying one of the park's milder diversions. After 1910, when tough anti-gambling laws shut down the Brooklyn racetracks, these ponies and Steeplechase's mechanical ones represented the only equine sport to be had on the island.

"Happy Children," Tilyou's Steeplechase Park. Coney Island, N.Y.

Come on and take a ride A.R.H.

These apparitions roamed through Steeplechase just as Mickey, Goofy & Co. do today in Disneyland. Some represented popular figures of the era—the sharply dressed bearded pair are supposed to be the great comic team of Weber and Fields—and the gargantuan turkey jittered about in celebration of the season's dance craze. The age was as diverted by the thought of the rube (the man holding the cane) squinting and stammering in the presence of urban progress as it was by the idea of a black policeman. Maggie Mahoney, the nine-foot-tall woman, is a mannequin, but the American Indian is almost certainly the real thing.

A GROUP OF FREAKS. FUNNY PLACE STEEPLECHASE. CONEY ISLAND. N. Y.

GEO. C. TILYOU'S STEEPLECHASE - FUNNY PLACE - WORLD'S FINEST CARROUSAL.

Any Coney Island advertising superlative is suspect, but there is a case for Tilyou's calling his carousel the world's finest. The magnificent El Dorado was born in Germany, made by Hugo Hasse, a Leipzig railroad bridge builder who also kept eight carnivals on tour and manufactured amusement devices. Seething with intricate carving, the forty-foot-high carousel had three tiers of platforms, each revolving at a different speed. It cost $150,000 to build and $30,000 in customs charges just to get it into the United States in 1910.

The El Dorado opened for business on West Fifth Street, where it made its presence known by the Ruth und Sohn band organ, whose voice could be heard clearly even on clangorous Surf Avenue. Tilyou got hold of the sumptuous machine in 1911 and moved it into his Pavilion of Fun. There it stayed for years, scintillating so splendidly that it gave rise to the legend—still irritating to carousel purists—that the finest merry-go-rounds inevitably came from Germany.

SCENE IN THE GARDEN, FUNNY PLACE STEEPLECHASE, CONEY ISLAND, N. Y.

There was a good deal more to Steeplechase than the Pavilion of Fun. Just
to the west was the garden, which Tilyou
called the Sunken Garden because that
sounded more enticing. The benches
there weren't electrified, and its fragrant
pathways soothed nerves strung too taut
by the thump and tumble of the Pavilion.

STEEPLE CHASE. SWIMMING POOL. BY NIGHT. CONEY ISLAND. N. Y.

The Sunken Garden lay between the Pavilion, which is glow-
ing to the far left in this picture, and the swimming pool.
Its plantings ran seaward to an airship ride and Tilyou's original
Ferris wheel. When he put up his wheel in 1896, ten thousand
people rode it every day. By 1910, when Steeplechase had
grown to be the elaborate institution shown on this card, the
wheel was old hat, and Tilyou had to drop the fare from a dime
to a nickel. But he was always proud of it, and liked to point
out that "it is lighted by 460 incandescent lights and can be
seen 38 miles at sea." Immigrants arriving from Europe saw
George C. Tilyou's Ferris wheel long before they caught their
first glimpse of the Statue of Liberty.

STEEPLECHASE, CONEY ISLAND.

Tilyou was less sentimental about his Giant See-Saw. For one thing, he hadn't built it. The ride had been put up at the 1901 Pan-American Exposition by Frederic Thompson and Elmer Dundy, and when Tilyou invited them to bring their Trip to the Moon to Steeplechase, the See-Saw came too.

The lunar voyage was a big draw, and it gave Tilyou a leg up on the competition during the ghastly season of 1902, which Coney Islanders remembered for decades as the summer that rain fell on seventy days in three months. But the next year, Tilyou cut Thompson and Dundy's share of the take from 60 to 40 percent.

The Coney Island historian Edo McCullough says that Tilyou did this to force the partners into building a park of their own, which would contribute to the greater glory of Coney Island. In assessing the veracity of this saintly motive, it is perhaps useful to remember that Tilyou was McCullough's uncle. In

any event, Thompson and Dundy got sore and said they were pulling out. They would take the Trip to the Moon with them, but they had no further use for the See-Saw. It had cost them $40,000. What would Tilyou pay?

"Let's toss for it, double or nothing."

Dundy aimed a coin at a crack in the floor; it rolled very close.

Tilyou fished a half-dollar out of his pocket and pitched it squarely on top of the crack.

"The See-Saw is yours," Dundy said. Then he asked if he could keep Tilyou's half-dollar to remember him by.

The ponderous See-Saw ran in Steeplechase only a few seasons before it became too costly to operate, but it stood for years, its great arm frozen a little off the horizontal, with the legend STEEPLE-CHASE spelled out across it in lights, surely the most arresting piece of advertising on the island.

And Thompson and Dundy went across the street to build Luna Park.

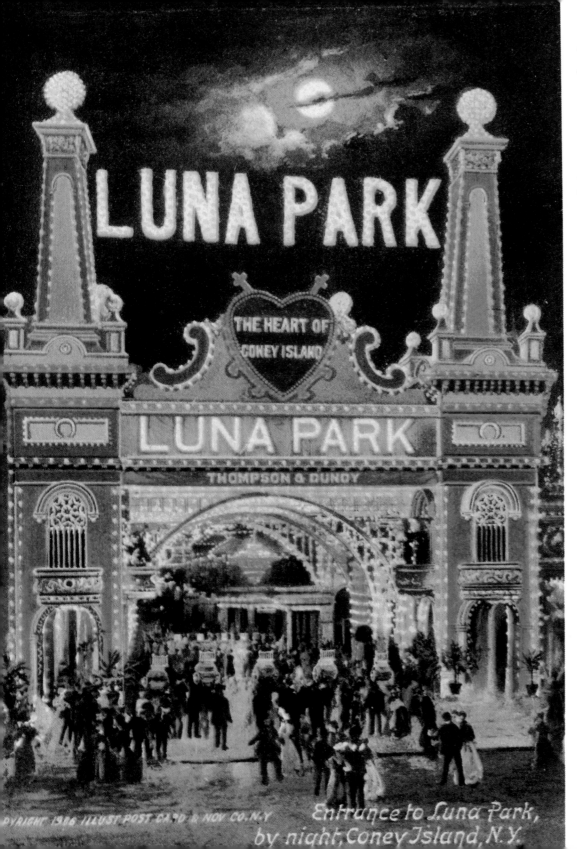

Entrance to Luna Park, by night, Coney Island, N.Y.

COPYRIGHT 1906 ILLUST POST CARD & NOV CO. N.Y

Luna Park opened for business at eight o'clock on the evening of May 16, 1903. Frederic Thompson and Elmer Dundy, its creators, doubtless picked that hour to get the most out of the cascades of electric light that were so much a part of the park's architecture. For weeks the partners had been running advertisements— "By day a paradise . . . At night, Arcadia"; "Electric Eden . . . Night as Noon-Tide"; "Harnessed Lightning in Flashing Fountains"—and now they would see whether the lights were bright enough to draw the crowds they needed.

Thompson and Dundy were broke. Their twenty-two-acre confection had cost far more than they'd planned; they liked to say $2,500,000, and in fact it may have come close to $1,000,000. The partners spent the day before the opening going around the island scrounging up change for the ticket booths.

They were able to borrow $22 in silver. It wasn't enough. When the gates opened that first night, 43,000 people teemed in, the change ran out, and thousands had to be admitted free. Thompson and Dundy didn't mind: they were showmen enough to see that Luna Park was going to make them very rich.

By August 9 the partners had realized 90 percent of their original investment. Some indication of Luna's success can be seen in the brief show-business career of Charles Murray, a Tilyou employee who cast his lot with Thompson and Dundy and worked through the summer without salary on a percentage basis. At the end of the first season he came away with $116,000 and immediately retired.

"Buildings," said Frederic Thompson, "can laugh quite as loudly as human beings." And if you're building an amusement park, you'd better see that they do: "A beautiful but excited sky-line is more important to an exposition than the correct demonstration of any man's recollection of the fine points of Sir Christopher Wren's handiwork!"

In setting out to design Luna, Thompson chose to "depart from all set rules of architecture except those which have to do with proportion and good taste." After all, architecture was nothing more nor less than scenery, and "it would never occur to you to invest 'The Pirates of Penzance' with the scenic background of a Western mining-camp." For an amusement park, "a spirit of frolic must be manufactured, and it cannot dwell where straight lines, dignified columns, and conventional forms predominate." Instead, Thompson reached back to the "grotesquely delightful" Aladdin-spires of childhood picture books, built them tall—the central tower was fully twenty stories high—and strung them together with flower-topped colonnades.

The effect was just what he had hoped. When Albert Bigelow Paine first saw Luna, he stopped, filled with "profound amazement," at the entrance gates: "Beyond . . . [was] an enchanted, story-book land of trellises, columns, domes, minarets, lagoons, and lofty aërial flights. And everywhere was life—a pageant of happy people; and everywhere was color—a wide harmony of orange and white and gold, under the cloudless blue."

8057. IN LUNA PARK, CONEY ISLAND, N. Y.   COPYRIGHT, 1905, BY DETROIT PUBLISHING CO.

Luna Park did its best to look like a storybook Baghdad, but it was a regular working city nonetheless. Every showman loved to throw out numbers. Here are the ones Frederic Thompson had at his command in the summer of 1909: Luna employed 1,500 people, 200 horses, 25 elephants and other animals; it added to the Coney Island skyline 1,214 "towers, minarets and spires"; operated its own wireless station, machine shop, and sawmill.

Getting in shape for the season had required: $400,000; eight carloads of paint (that's *box*car loads); 1,200,000 electric lightbulbs; 70,000 palms and plants; 10,000 new flags; 720,000 linear feet of lumber.

The elephants and their colleagues performed on a platform in the middle of the lagoon. Dundy handled the financial end of things, but he had imposed one creative stipulation on Thompson: he loved circuses, and Luna must have one.

Thompson knew what he was doing when he called Luna the Electric Eden: the prodigal application of electricity was as fascinating as any show or ride to turn-of-the-century audiences. *Scientific American* said approvingly that at Coney Island, in 1910, "enough light is being used to illuminate a city of five hundred thousand souls."

At night Luna's every bulge and spike was defined by strings of light bulbs— "sketched in flame," the journalists liked to say—and although this picture has been embellished with the addition of prettily painted crowds, a turbulent au-tumnal sky, and apocryphal American flags, the feeling is right.

The molten globe in the lower center of the picture is a scale: if the operator guessed your weight wrong, you paid nothing (but it only happened when he wanted to encourage the crowd). To the right is a lemonade stand armed, one customer said, "with rows of thick glasses two thirds full of salmon and chrome colored beverages, which at some stage of their evolution have been on terms of bowing acquaintance with oranges and lemons."

COPYRIGHT 1904 BY LUNA PARK CO.
A trip to the moon, in the world famous air ship "Luna".—LUNA PARK, NEW YORK.

Luna Park issued handsome lithograph cards of its top attractions at the start of its second season. The Trip to the Moon had been Thompson and Dundy's original hit at the Pan-American Exposition and subsequently at Steeplechase, and it kept right on packing them in at Luna. In fact, most people thought the park took its name from this, its germinal attraction; actually, it had been christened after Thompson's partner's sister, Luna Dundy.

The illusion may not have been quite as sweeping as the card suggests, but it was impressive nonetheless. Passengers climbed into an airship whose captain stepped forth to announce that soon they'd be "skimming the cream from the Milky Way." Then, said one voyager, "The great wings lifted and fell, the aerodrome heaved, the earth dropped down from sight, and we felt that we were soaring far above on our lunar journey. Suddenly there was a darkening, followed by complete blackness. Lightning flashed across the sky. Thunder rolled and crashed, and there was fierce rain on the awning overhead."

"We are passing through a storm," the captain would shout. "We are quite safe." Sure enough, the thunderstorm died away, leaving the night sky peppered with stars. They began to dim as dawn came on, and the surface of the moon loomed up, pink with morning light.

This sublime moment was somewhat mitigated by the moonmen, who came capering around the departing passengers waving pieces of green cheese and shrilling out selections from the endless repertory of popular songs with the word "moon" in the title.

The evolution of the Iron Clad, shown in the production of War is Hell.—LUNA PARK, NEW YORK

Despite the card's rather pious caption, this attraction was not a cautionary historical examination of the development of seapower. It was, rather, a bit of cheerful pandering to the national mood during America's first decade as an imperial presence.

Originally called Thompson & Dundy's Great Naval Spectatorium, and soon given the more wieldy name War of the Worlds, the show had a simple plot. The audience, seated in what was said to be one of the batteries guarding New York Harbor, saw the combined navies of the world—Germany and Britain, France and Spain—steam up over the horizon sixty strong and begin to close on Manhattan.

But before they could work any of their devilish foreign mischief, the American fleet swung out in line of battle and sank every single one of them.

This exhibition was described as "Startling, Stupendous, Soul-Stirring" by its owners, who observed, "It will no doubt gratify President Roosevelt and Admiral Dewey to have demonstrated here the fact that New York is impregnable and that the allied navies of the world could not in safety pass the American forts."

A couple of seasons later, with the adaptability necessary to commercial survival on Coney, the show was transformed into the Russo-Japanese war battle of Port Arthur.

SHOOTING THE CHUTES, CONEY ISLAND, N. Y.

2054.   ILLUST. POST. CARD CO., N. Y.

The Shoot the Chutes, a holdover from Boyton's original Sea Lion Park, never lost its popularity. There could be no simpler ride: a half-dozen people climbed into a flat-bottomed barge, which slid down a watery incline and skipped out into a lake, to be hooked in by a waiting bargeman. The critic James Huneker dismissed the experience as being "shot down a chute into irritated water." But generations of visitors invoked the Shoot the Chutes as a sort of generic symbol of all the pleasures Coney had to offer.

Shooting the Chutes, Coney Island, N. Y.

70-66

One boat has nearly reached the starting point; another rumbles lakeward while the bargeman stands swaying in the stern with the contemptuous ease of the old salt. Everybody is smiling; everybody always smiled on the Chutes. Rupert Hughes, who was so scornful of the Steeplechase horses, was stirred by "the shoot-the-chutes, where one felt the rapture of a seagull swooping to the waves—the long, swift glide down the wet incline, and the glorious splash into the flying spray!—who would not rather be a gondolier on one of those flatboats than Admiral Makaroff? or the latest flying machinist who spattered to the ground?"

TRIP TO MARS, LUNA PARK, CONEY ISLAND, N.Y.

TRIP TO MARS
BY AEROPLANE

LANDING STATION
AERIAL NAVIGATION CO.
A TRIP TO MARS

Showmen needed to keep up with the times. A Trip to the Moon was fine in the summer of 1903 when the Wright Brothers had yet to fly. But by 1912, when this card was posted, a more ambitious trip was in order: after all, Cal Rogers had already made a Trip to California by Aeroplane, made it in eighty-four days and five crashes after taking off on September 17, 1911, from Coney Island.

Luna Park was full of elephants. Both partners liked elephants, and when they opened the Hippodrome in New York, the columns were topped with elephant heads. But for some reason, the people who went to Coney in the first decade of the century seemed to be far more taken with camels.

"Oh, that camel!" wrote Guy Wetmore Carryl, out for the day at the expense of *Munsey's* magazine. "Once ship of the desert, decked in gaudy trappings and bearing his Arab master at breakneck speed across a sea of sand: what a derelict for any one to mount upon he is now become! The long, laborious course from Wara to Mourzouk has dwindled to a bare half-hundred yards, but these he traverses as many times a day, rising and crouching again with protesting snorts, a sneer on his long lower lip, and a resentful gleam in his formerly patient eyes. He knows, though we do not, the proper way in which to mount and to descend, and he has yet to see it exemplified at Coney Island."

"Poor beasts!" said Elmer Blaney Harris, surveying them with Dora. "Relics of ancient philosophies, enduring Americanitis with supercilious patience."

Dora was less philosophical; she merely said, "Going up," got herself "perched, taking a firm hold, and then winked back. Up got Holy Moses, tail first, and off they paraded."

Coney Island
LUNA PARK - Helter Skelter

The Helter Skelter was as popular as the Chutes. "The passengers," said Elmer Blaney Harris, "are lifted on an automatic stairway to the top of the high tower, where an attendant gives each a door mat. The mat is welcome, whether it says so or not. This they adjust under them and down the slide they go, head first or heels first, as it pleases them. . . . The descent itself is about fifty feet, with high sides, like a bathtub, and it twists and turns suddenly, a man standing guard at the bottom to pick up the passengers. A fat woman came to a standstill at one of the turns, and it required the combined impetus of the next four to dislodge her. Dora's only comment was:

" 'I'm never going to eat another potato!' "

Like Tilyou, Frederic Thompson understood the enduring popularity of his simpler rides. An elaborate theatrical production was always a gamble; the Helter Skelter wasn't.

"That," said Thompson, "is just the old sliding down the cellar door. In sheer amusement, as distinct from entertainments, youngsters and oldsters are precisely alike; we must not do something for them, we must give them something to do."

HELTER SKELTER, LUNA PARK, CONEY ISLAND, N.Y.

127 The Tickler at Luna Park, Coney Island.

"Best of all—the Tickler." This was the finest forty seconds Elmer and Dora had on Coney: "This unique device is the most surprising, the most disconcerting . . . of any on the Island. We laughed at the tubfuls of unfortunates until Dora, catching the fever, tightened her hairpins and declared she would try her luck. . . . Before we had time to reconsider we were seated in the tub and on our way up, facing half a dozen others all getting a strangle hold. The tubs are on casters, allowing them to play the deuce with direction. . . . We reached the top and away we went. As one soon finds, unless the neck is kept rigid one's head may be snapped from one's shoulders. We descended in a sort of reverse English, hanging on for dear life. . . . Dora was the star performer. She early lost her grip, and in my efforts to keep her in the seat I lost mine. Like a couple of shuttlecocks we were battered around in the bottom of the car. . . ."

Guy Wetmore Carryl, who had no Dora with him, was appalled to "be packed in a monster barrel and be rolled incontinently down a hill. . . . There are milder things than that barrel shown in European museums in execration of the Spanish Inquisition."

Stranger, perhaps, than any lunar voyage or make-believe war was the Candy Delicatessen. This astonishing concern sold—and the list is worth running in its entirety—"Sauer Kraut, Frankfurters, Pork Sausages, Winter Bologna, Liver Pudding, Blood Pudding, Ham Bologna, Salami, Cervelat, Breaded Veal Cutlets, Pork Chops, Fish Cakes, Sweet Potatoes, New Spuds, Fruits and Vegetables, Cheese, Deviled Crabs, Deviled Clams, Fried Oysters, Chicken Croquettes, Meat Balls, Plum Pudding and a great many others, too numerous to mention, all made of Pure Candy."

Marietta Holley, in one of the humorous dialect novels the era inexplicably cherished, told of coming from the country to visit Luna and seeing "a big butcher shop, with hull sides of beef, mutton, pork, hams, chickens, etc., hangin' up. And a long counter, piled full of invitin' lookin' pieces ready to roast or brile. . . . Everything looked good and clean, but I'd hearn of city meat givin' toe main pizen, and . . . I asked anxiously, 'Are you sure the critters this meat come from hadn't got cow consumption or hog cholera?'"

"Every mite of that is candy," a woman explained: "And she offered me a piece of sassidge, and asked which I preferred, wintergreen or peppermint."

359   QUAINT PEOPLE AT LUNA PARK, New York.   Copyright by C. H. Murray.

Luna's "quaint people" included Hawaiians, East Indian natives, and stoic Eskimos with their sled dogs.

People from the Indies; people from the Arctic; Transvaal guerrillas hammering it out with British regulars; camels; elephants; the Alps; the North Pole. . . . Between June and September Coney was, as George C. Tilyou said, the World.

In his story "A Lickpenny Lover," O. Henry has Irving Carter, "painter, millionaire, traveller, poet, automobilist," enter a Manhattan department store, spot the beautiful Masie behind the glove counter, and instantly fall in love.

Two weeks later, the rich boy proposes: "Marry me, Masie, and we will go away from this ugly city to beautiful ones. . . . Just think of a shore where summer is eternal, where the waves are always rippling on the lovely beach and the people are happy and free as children. We will sail to those shores. . . .

"After the European cities we will visit India and the ancient cities there, and ride on elephants and see the wonderful temples of the Hindoos and Brahmins and the Japanese gardens and the camel trains and chariot races in Persia, and all the queer sights of foreign countries. Don't you think you would like it, Masie?"

"I think we had better be going home," she says, and the next day, back behind the counter, she tells her friend Lulu her suitor is out of the picture. " 'What do you think that fellow wanted me to do?' "

" 'Go on the stage?' guessed Lulu, breathlessly.

" 'Nit; he's too cheap a guy for that. He wanted me to marry him and go down to Coney Island for a wedding tour!' "

91

The grandest and most elaborate of all Coney Island's parks was the child of Luna's success. Thompson and Dundy cleared $600,000 at the end of their first season. That kind of profit was extremely interesting to Senator Paul Reynolds, and he set about raising an investment group to build a rival park.

The result was Dreamland, tall, white, splendid—and always exhaling the smell of political jobbery. Reynolds was a high roller whose friends—Big Tim Sullivan the Tammany boss and state senator Pat McCarren, who ran Brooklyn—had no trouble getting the New York Board of Estimate to turn over West Eighth Street to them gratis when they bought the two strips of land that ran alongside it from Surf Avenue to the Atlantic. Dreamland's foundations went down before the city could take away its fire hydrants (years later, the park would be accused of using city water in its shows and rides), and by the spring of 1904 workmen were putting the final coat of white paint on the park's walls and towers.

Architecturally, Dreamland was more sophisticated than its rivals, as is suggested by this entrance, which led, also, to a Biblical spectacular called Creation. The spread wings not only formed the entrance but, by rendering the great welcoming figure allegorical, made her bare breasts acceptable to the era.

2010   DREAMLAND ENTRANCE, CONEY ISLAND, N. Y.

8962.   TWILIGHT, DREAMLAND, CONEY ISLAND, N. Y.

Here is Dreamland at the hour that is most beguiling in any amusement park, when the pulse of the long afternoon slows a little and the lights begin to come on. This card was printed by the Detroit Publishing Company, which took pains to make its reproduction crisp and the colors accurate. Its efforts were particularly effective here, and this scene looking north from Dreamland's chutes toward Surf Avenue and, at the left, Luna Park, is perhaps the best and truest postcard view there is of Coney Island at the peak of its career.

Dreamland was designed by the New York architectural firm of Kirby, Petit and Green, and during the park's first season the critic Barr Feree subjected it to a long and serious evaluation in *Architects' and Builders' Magazine*. He had some reservations, but in the main he found Dreamland a splendid success. He was especially impressed by the 375-foot central tower: "Large in size, it is so admirably proportioned as to be the commanding feature without any sense of grossness. The windows that fill the centre of its four sides are amply buttressed by the solid piers of the corners; and the crowning member is very happy, a fine pyramidal effect being obtained by a very judicious retreating and recessing of parts to the ball and eagle on the summit. The archways at the base are also well managed; they are large enough to give a needed sense of openness and yet not so large as to interfere with the equally necessary sense of stability required at the base of so lofty a structure. . . .

"The tower is the dominant note of Dreamland. It raises its graceful head far above the structures of Coney Island, and . . . doubtless fulfills very competently every possible requirement of an advertisement; it is much more to the point, from the present point of view, that whatever be its organic function, it is a fine structure in itself, very goodly to look upon."

The author of *Seeing Coney Island* would have found Feree's assessment pretty timid; according to that 1904 guidebook, Dreamland's central spire was simply "the finest tower ever built."

CASH GIRLS, DREAMLAND.
CONEY ISLAND.

Dreamland's aspirations toward gentili-ty are clearly evident in this early-morning scene of the cash girls, each in the cap and gown of a college graduate, going to their posts past the Ionic col-umns on the facade of the Fall of Pom-peii Building. Inside, it was the same old blood and thunder; outside, some-thing rare enough in an amusement park: "behind the columns," wrote Barr Feree in his critique, "a superb view of the Bay of Naples has been painted by the well-known decorative artist, Mr. Charles M. Shean. This is one of the most nota-ble pieces of mural decoration in this country, being painted on the actual plas-ter, whereas most work of this description is done on canvass by the artist in the privacy of his studio." Shean, however, came out to Coney and, with a single assistant to help him, finished his fresco in just nine days. "But there is no hint of haste or speed in it; the color is good, and the picture thoroughly redeems and ennobles a building that, without it, would attract little attention."

Despite its blandness, Feree thought the Pompeii Building had "considerable dignity." Next to it, however, stood a structure of real imagination. The Electri-city Building, at the right of the picture, housed the generators that lit the park's one million electric lights, and its facade was shaped like the armature of a dynamo.

In further tribute to Western cultural tradition, Dreamland offered what Feree called a "free rendering" of the Doge's Palace in Venice. In fact, it was quite a careful piece of archaeology, and had to be: reverent imitations of Renaissance palaces were being built as private homes all over Manhattan, and people were starting to have a pretty good idea of what the real article was supposed to look like.

Inside the Doge's Palace, gondolas floated along a watery path while Venetian scenes jostled gently past. "The soft moonlight typical of the city," said a guidebook, was "shed by a newly invented electrical device." Both these cards are actual photographs of the ride's interior, but they have been heavily doctored in a not altogether successful attempt to remove the impression of a low ceiling.

Dreamland: Fighting the Flames. Coney Island, N.Y.

Dreamland drew not only on the classical tradition for its attractions, but on Luna Park as well. Luna had a successful show in which firefighters saved a burning building. Dreamland appropriated the idea, inflated it, and put it behind this imposing facade with its sculpted firemen.

The result disgusted one critic, who wrote that "the year 1904 will be memorable, if for nothing else than those two terrible disasters, the burning of the Iroquois Theater and the excursion boat *General Slocum*. So great was the supposed revulsion on the part of the public after the first of these disasters that theatrical managers found it necessary to cut out any use of flames in a stage performance. . . . And yet, perhaps the two most successful shows at Coney Island last summer were the exhibitions, really terrible in their realism, of burning buildings, which seems to show that the morbid love of the public for devastating flames is just as great as it ever was. . . ."

"Trained fire-fighters attack sham conflagrations in a city block made of iron scenery," wrote one visitor, "after a rather elaborate acting out, by a crowd of two or three hundred people, of the life in a city street, just to make the display more realistic. The fire-engines are real, the water is real, and the leaps of men and women from the roofs of the buildings into the life-nets are real."

Here a hook-and-ladder truck, steam pumpers, and the fire chief's buggy have arrived on the scene to send a squadron of men crawling over the face of the threatened building. Dreamland publicists claimed that two thousand actors took part in the show, and whether or not that many really did turn out for the sham catastrophe, there was no denying that Dreamland's inflammable building was six stories high, while Luna's had only four.

MINIATURE RAILWAY, DREAMLAND, CONEY ISLAND.

The steam engines that threaded their way through the park were so literal that it seemed especially odd to see them pulling gold-and-scarlet gondolas instead of boxcars and daycoaches. The pretty little 4-4-0 locomotives, which were made by the Cagney Brothers' Miniature Railroad Company on lower Broadway, were powerful enough to pull up to ten tons at ten miles per hour. The Cagney company claimed they could earn $1,500 in less than a week.

Each park had its miniature railway, and in 1910, Hugh Thomas, Luna's electrical engineer, went Dreamland one better by replacing the live steamers in his park with electric locomotives. "The effect is extremely realistic," said *Scientific American*, "as the motors are encased in double-ended cabs such as are in use on many electrical railways of larger growth."

For all its aeroplane trips and submarine voyages, Luna may have been most prophetic in its abandonment of steam railroading.

100

The miniature railway ran past a miniature world. Here, in a dwindled Old Nuremberg of dark-red peaked roofs and somber masonry walls, lived a colony of midgets, with their own circus, music hall, police force, and fire department, which dashed to false alarms hourly.

Samuel Gumpertz drummed up the three hundred little people necessary to populate this doggedly fanciful place. He did not find the chore particularly taxing.

Gumpertz could go anywhere and get anything. Born in St. Louis in 1868, he worked as an acrobat before he was ten years old, and went on to serve as a candy butcher, a performer in Buffalo Bill's Wild West, a manager of prizefighters, actors, movie companies (he salvaged the profits of a Russian coronation newsreel by renaming it "The Great Bradley Martin Ball" after a scandalously expensive New York society party), and amusement parks.

Senator Reynolds made him manager of Dreamland. In 1905 he imported 212 Bantoc tribesmen from the Philippines, and after that, he never stopped. During his life Gumpertz shepherded some 3,800 people into the United States; he went five times to Asia, five times to Africa, and anywhere in the world where he thought he could lay hands on a diverting aborigine or a freak. He was rarely stumped: he never did find an honest example of that ubiquitous sideshow fixture the Half-Man-Half-Woman; but he had no trouble recruiting the inhabitants of Midget City.

CARTER & GUT, PUBLISHERS, N.Y.

MRS. GENERAL TOM THUMB (Countess Magré) and
Count Magré's residence, Midget City, Dreamland, Coney Island

The Count and Countess Magri (the
card's spelling of the name is refined but
inaccurate) were Midget City's leading
citizens. The count's title had been bestowed on him by the Pope, and appar-
ently he was secure enough in it to toler-
ate good-humoredly his wife's obvious de-
votion to her first husband. The thirty-
two-inch-tall Mercy Lavinia Warren Bump
had married the count back in 1885, but
she spoke constantly of the great days
when she and her first husband had been
received by President and Mrs. Lincoln,
and she continued to bill herself as Mrs.
General Tom Thumb.

THE ANIMAL AVALANCHE

FRANK C. BOSTOCK
THE ANIMAL KING

MLLE. AURORA AND HER POLAR BEARS

Dear You must go to "Bostock's." it is certainly the best show on Coney Island. Yours

Housed in a large and, according to Feree, "pretentious" building facing the tower, Bostock's animal show was Dreamland's answer to Carl Hagenbeck's circus in Luna. Along with Mlle. Aurora's bears and the animal avalanche, the audience could see Madame Morelli with her seven leopards and Herman Weedom with an assortment of tigers, pumas, hyenas, and other animals which, one unreceptive witness said, had been "tortured into talent." Here, as at the Rough Riders scenic railway, the management offered patrons the convenience of a postcard that had merely to be signed: the message was provided.

Capt. Jack Bonavita and the lion "Baltimore".

FRANK C. BOSTOCK
THE ANIMAL KING

Dear you must go to "Bostock's" it certainly is the best show on Coney Island. Yours Mother!

Captain Jack Bonavita was Bostock's biggest draw. No lion tamer ever put on a better show. After one of his cats took a swipe at his hand that cost him two fingers, the convalescing captain would push himself out in a wheelchair for each performance and sit glaring at his caged attacker. The hand got infected. Gumpertz posted daily medical bulletins on Surf Avenue in front of Dreamland. Finally, Bonavita lost his right arm—which doubled his popularity when he returned to the ring.

Elmer Blaney Harris watched him work: "Silence. The bravest of Bostock's protégés was in the arena, driving Baltimore to his perch against the bars. Nine other tawny noblemen of the jungle sat round, licking their chops. Inch by inch the man-eater gave way before the lash that spat into his eye. Now and then, as the whip bit closer, there came a flash of fangs, a sidewise crouch, and a blur as the lion threatened the trainer with his fist. He turned once and delivered—the nine others pointed their heads—but he missed. Baffled, humiliated, still muttering his defiance, he deliberately took his place—and the man had won. In the audience women relaxed and fanned; men dried the palms of their hands and shook a smile at one another."

Those who found this kind of primal confrontation too heady could step across to Wormwood's Monkey Theater, where "The Greatest Aggregation of Educated Animals on Earth"—125 ant-eaters, chickens, monkeys and lemurs—performed a three-act drama entitled "The Pardon Came Too Late."

103

12701 Dreamland and Luna Park from the top of the Dreamland Chutes, Coney Island.

It is fully dark now, and we are looking across Dreamland to where Luna Park blazes away beyond the dim Channel of Surf Avenue.

All this electrical coruscation enchanted visitors when they first saw it, but a day on Coney that stretched into night tended to leave them jaded. People found they had spent a dollar more than planned; they were queasy from eating what one called "retrospective" seafood; the genial fizz of the beer consumed under the leaves at Feltman's was gone; and in the glare, at once impersonal and intimate, that brought the black sky down close overhead, the sinister element that is part of any amusement park became more insistent. Ahead lay the long trip home. The frankfurter and taffy stands that were not near the steamboat pier or the railroad depots began putting up their shutters.

Elmer Blaney Haris was alone again. Dora had said to him, "Come on, now, dance!" and they'd gone to the big Dreamland ballroom, out on the end of the old Iron Pier. "Although prepared for much, I was surprised at the grace with which she danced. She didn't wish to be held in the prevailing fashion, tight and affectionately; nor was the slow half-time at all to her liking. She gave me but the tips of her fingers . . . [and] succeeded in making me feel that I was in no wise necessary, merely useful as an escort. Imagine my surprise, therefore, when, at the close of the encore, she suddenly, with a little purr, flung both arms around my neck and kissed me lightly on the cheek.

" 'Oh, look!' she cried, pointing over my shoulder.

"I looked. And when I turned back—she was gone—swallowed up in that impenetrable crowd. I laughed at her ruse,

both amused and chagrined by her impromptu goodby—or was it premeditated? While still revolving it in my mind, I reached the gates of the Park. An "L" was just pulling out from the station. And there, hands folded on the window ledge, was Dora, her hat off, looking at the lights of the Park in a kind of serene indifference to it, to me, and to all else about her. The train increased its speed, turned a corner—and that was the last of Dora. . . ."

Harris wandered disconsolately onto the Bowery. "All evening long the exits had been draining the Island until now there was little left but scum. Midnight sounded. The parks shut down. The Tower in Dreamland closed its fifty thousand eyes."

As the parks blinked out, the bad old Coney that everybody said was gone pressed in on Harris. "The fun in the lesser resorts became diseased. Piano playing and tipsy laughter flooded the concert halls magnetized by a horseshoe of tired females trading jests with a masculine audience. Here and there, a few steps off the beaten path encumbered with ruins of celebration—corncobs gnawed clean like bones, trampled rind of watermelon, muddied candy bags, and refuse from a day's dishwashing upon the curb—were snap-shots in low doorways of disheveled women and men in shirtsleeves, a gray helmeted policeman, club swinging, alert in the shadow."

The great pleasure engines dark and silent behind him, Harris walked out across the beach past couples sleeping in each other's arms. It was too late to go home, too early to go anywhere else. At the edge of the surf, he stripped naked and waded out into the incorruptible Atlantic.

In his interminable denunciation of Coney Island, Maxim Gorky dismissed a tour through a papier-mâché netherworld with "Hell is very badly done."

But Hell was not badly done the night before the Memorial Day weekend of 1911.

The weekend was the official opening of the season at Coney. If the day was fair, 200,000 people would spill onto Surf Avenue with money to spend, and the concessionaires had to be ready for them.

At Hell Gate, in Dreamland, workmen were up late caulking a leak in one of the sluices that carried boatloads of riders toward the ultimate tin whirlpool. A little before two in the morning of May 27, the circuitry that was the park's pride began to act up. Light bulbs near the workmen exploded; someone spilled a bucket of hot tar, and in minutes Hell Gate and its brooding devil were in flames.

CONEY ISLAND'S BIGGEST FIRE DISASTER
TRYING TO SAVE LIONS · · · ·
· · · · · · ·DURING THE FIRE.

Half an hour after the first alarm, the Dreamland tower was a torch visible in Manhattan, and the fire had reached the animals. Burning parrots looped shrieking through the air, and the big cats began fighting each other.

Captain Bonavita had been asleep in an apartment in the animal house. "I heard pounding and beating on the doors below. I knew something very serious was going on, so I sprang up and put on my slippers and smoking jacket. I never heard such commotion among wild animals. . . . Everything downstairs was in confusion. The electric lights wouldn't work. My eight helpers came with lanterns. By the fitful light of these we tried to drive the crazed beasts into the great arena cage. They snarled and cowered in corners, biting and worrying the bars. The smoke got more and more difficult to stand. . . ."

Many animals died screaming in their cages; some got into the auditorium and escaped to the street. Black Prince, a three-year-old Nubian lion, ran burning onto Surf Avenue and into the Rocky Road to Dublin. Trainers and policemen followed the bleeding, terrified animal up the steep tracks of the scenic railway to the roof, where they shot him dead on the plaster battlements.

Working in scalding darkness, Bonavita and his men managed to get five leopards and four lions—one of them the pregnant Victoria—into movable cages and pulled them to safety.

This highly daring rescue was reconstructed by a postcard manufacturer as soon as he got wind of it, and this card was for sale before the ashes had cooled.

CONEY ISLAND'S BIGGEST FIRE DISASTER
PANORAMIC VIEW OF THE RUINS OF
BURNED DISTRICT

A little after three o'clock, the Dreamland tower folded in on itself and sank through clouds of molten froth. The fire chief on the scene pulled in a double-nine alarm; it was the first time in Brooklyn's history that so urgent a call had been issued, and it brought in pumpers from eight miles away.

Thirty-three fire companies had gotten to Coney, but still the fires burned: L. A. Thompson's Oriental Scenic Railway and his Pike's Peak Railway both disappeared; then the Great Whirlwind coaster went up in flames; and finally the Observation Tower, that relic of the Centennial, caught fire too.

Eventually the flames were brought to a halt at West Fifth Street—more by the wind than by the fire engines—and although the paint blistered on the Galveston Flood Building, it survived the night.

By the time the sun rose into a cloudless sky, the firemen were packing up and heading for home. More than four hundred men had fought the fire, among them the members of the Midget City Fire Department, who, when the real thing came down upon them after all their hundreds of false alarms, battled gamely with their miniature steam pumpers to save Old Nuremberg.

But in the end, the grandest of Coney Island's parks disappeared entirely, leaving nothing save incandescent rubble and a sweet, haunting little waltz called "Meet Me Tonight in Dreamland," which had been written to celebrate the park's opening just six seasons earlier.

Dreamland Circus,
Coney Island, N. Y.

Samuel Gumpertz stood as close to the fire as he could bear, watching the park he managed die its spectacular death. At one point Frederic Thompson walked over and wordlessly shook his hand.

Gumpertz was a showman, and when the reporters questioned him, he promptly replied, "The public may be sure that a greater and finer Dreamland is going to rise from these ashes."

But Senator Reynolds, who would be the man to do the building, thought differently: "The loss is about $2,125,000," he said, "of which $400,000 was covered by insurance. I don't know what we will do until the board of directors meets, but I don't think we should be permitted to rebuild. There is too much risk."

In the end, what rose from the ashes of Dreamland was this freak show. It belonged to Gumpertz. He rallied his human skeletons and wild men and giants around him in the wake of the disaster, and had them under canvas putting on a show so soon after the fire that they complained about the heat of the debris underfoot.

In time Gumpertz was running the operation pictured here: very fancy by sideshow standards, but a paltry successor to Dreamland.

In 1905, Lindsay Denison had written, "Because it is still new in its present form [Coney Island] is as yet a city of frame and staff, relying on its show fire departments and on tin sheeting to protect itself from a disastrous blaze. But as profits are turned into invested capital, brick and stone will take the place of the flimsier materials. . . . The playhouse will become a permanent temple of fun for the people."

But Coney was still frame and staff in 1911, and every year thereafter Lindsay Denison's marble temple of fun receded a little further into improbability.

Subway and Elevated Stations, Coney Island, N. Y.

EPILOGUE

The subway reached Coney after World War I. Now that anyone could get there for a nickel, the summer crowds grew from a quarter million a day to a million. This new clientele hadn't as much money to spend as the old. A young man named Nathan Handwerker saw what was coming and, after a year of slicing hot-dog rolls at Feltman's, he took his $300 savings and leased the corner of a building on Surf Avenue. There he sold pineapple drink for three cents, ice-cream sodas for eight cents—and hot dogs for a nickel. Feltman's held firm at a traditional price of a dime. Nathan Handwerker's fortunes rose.

Frederic Thompson's declined. His park survived the great fire, but the next year he lost it anyway. A few seasons earlier he had had a personal fortune of $1,500,000; but his partner, Elmer Dundy, died in 1907, and Thompson's hold began to slip. He drank too much. In 1912 he went into bankruptcy, $664,000 in debt. "It's proof I'm no piker, isn't it," he said. He stayed on as manager of Luna for a while, went to California in hopes of recapturing his old success, failed, and came back East to die in 1919.

Luna Park kept going, but the old formulas began to fail. People had stood in line to see the fantasy battle between the American fleet and the navies of the world; but now that there had been a real War of the Worlds, nobody seemed to want to watch a reenactment: a cyclorama of the Battle of the Marne that was set up in the old Trip to the Moon building did dismally. Luna decayed during the 1930s, held on through the Second World War, and was finally done in by a series of fires in the late 1940s.

The crowds were changing; the island was changing. Still, the new generations came to Steeplechase; Tilyou's durable formula outlasted the Depression and the war. When television came in, Steeplechase Park set up a television theater with half a dozen screens, each permanently tuned in to a different channel. Elderly ladies would come in the afternoon and sit there tranquilly in front of their favorite shows, while the machines they'd ridden half a century before rattled away behind them.

But in the end, Steeplechase closed too. The park failed to open for the 1965 season. A scant decade or so before the burgeoning historic preservation movement might have saved the glass-and-cast-iron building, the Trump Corporation pulled it apart to develop real estate, developed no real estate, and eventually sold the level patch of cinders to the city.

Whatever it had once done for people, Coney no longer did. Perhaps the controlled violence of its mechanical rides and the shows that brought the world into a few acres of shorefront had made the real world seem less perilous; and perhaps television was doing that now. In any event, the amusement district drew in on itself until it straddled only a few blocks of Surf Avenue. Urban-renewal projects clawed apart the nearby neighborhoods, then ran out of money. "The neighborhoods have been torn up, made worse than they were, and forsaken," said one longtime resident in 1976. "It is a great dumping ground."

On a cold, cloudy day early last spring, the old Coney had dwindled almost out of existence. The western end of the amusement district was anchored, as it had been since Steeplechase Park died, by Nathan Handwerker's refreshment stand, which has grown into Nathan's Famous. Even on this windy, wintry morning, cars were stopped two deep in front of Nathan's while the drivers scuttled to the curb to buy french fries and soda and the sometime nickel hot dog, which now costs $1.15.

But behind Nathan's the sense of living commerce disappeared. Here the scabby, sagging remnants of the Bowery stretched a few blocks east to where a wretched ride called Spookarama inexplicably survived.

The thundery light gave everything the same visual weight, so that the cheap flashing on the surviving buildings shone, and the cream-and-red lettering on the Thunderbolt, bright with its varnish of rainwater, still radiated the old fun. But the tracks leading to the incline were submerged, and although the wooden latticework looked strong, the coaster seemed derelict.

Between it and the ocean the huge, pale-blue spokes of a newer failed ride lay sunk in sand and rubble, looking like wreckage left behind after a war with Mars. So many of the buildings along the shore had vanished that there was more sense of the ocean at Coney than there had been for at least eighty years.

On this clammy spring day, the Cyclone coaster and the Wonder Wheel, two steel products of the 1920s that are good for many seasons more, looked not only abandoned, but curiously industrial, as though their job was cracking polymers rather than diverting people.

The Coney Island of the postcards was evident only in the humblest remnants: a gray wooden cornice, a brief run of arches, the Bowery itself.

There is more of Caesar's Rome left than there is of Tilyou's Coney. But people remember.

George C. Tilyou died in 1914, his park in 1964; and yet on the nearest standing wall there was a spanking new mural done by an organization called the Coney Island Hysterical Society. Nicely painted, it showed the Steeplechase man and his smile inside the park's circular combination ticket, in front of a handsome rendering of the building itself, and the legend:

"Steeplechase Park . . .

Come Back . . .

Come Back . . ."

Beyond the mural, the Bowery lay wet and steely, innocent even of garbage. Suddenly, through that disconsolate street, there came like sunlight the virile boom and chatter of a carousel band organ—no recording, but the real thing: bellows blowing through a roll of perforated paper, setting pipes hooting and wooden hammers vibrating.

It was coming from the B & B Carousell. That is how William Mangels used to spell the word, and the operator of the Surf Avenue merry-go-round said that Mangels had indeed built it.

It was pleasant to think that he had been the builder of the old Coney's lustiest survivor. Mangels had a shop right over on West Fifth Street, where he turned out shooting galleries and striking machines, and bigger stuff: he invented the Tickler and brought it to Frederic Thompson, and he made the Ziz coaster for Charles Feltman, and the Rough Riders coaster. But he was especially proud of his "Galloping Horse Carousells," whose "system of decoration—the extensive use of beveled mirrors—is being universally approved," and whose "patent overhead transmission with direct gear connection" gave the horses "a beautiful gliding motion . . . unlike the old style, where the horses only have a slight rocking motion."

William Mangels outlived all his friends in the business at Coney—Thompson and Tilyou, Stauch and Henderson and Gumpertz—and toward the end of his life he wanted to commemorate what they'd done there. He tried to found a museum of public recreation, and when that failed he wrote a solemn and appealing book called *A History of the Outdoor*

Amusement Industry, which he published in 1952.

And now, under the close gray sky, it was his Galloping Horse Carousell that was fighting a solitary rear-guard action against whatever Coney Island may become.

The rain came down, the sidewalks were deserted, but the band organ sang out "Over the Waves," and the horses lifted and fell, lifted and fell, moving forward through the stormlight.

Stauch's Entrance to Dance Hall
CONEY ISLAND

117

QUALITY

Geo. C. Tilyou's
STEEPLECHASE PARK
Coney Island, N. Y.

Is the largest and the most completely equipped FUN FACTORY in the world.

Containing 2 SWIMMING POOLS, OCEAN BATHING BEACH, BALL ROOM, ROLLER SKATING RING, besides THE GREAT PAVILION OF FUN.

115157